Collins
MUSIC

C000260779

How to teach
Secondary
Music

100
INSPIRING IDEAS

Anh Doan and David Guinane

Table of contents

How to use this book

Dip into this book whenever you want a flash of inspiration to improve and inspire your music teaching.

The ideas in this book are organised by theme – these are given at the foot of each page. Each idea follows a very simple format:

○ Title: the catchy title sums up what the idea is about.

○ Quote: the opening quote from a teacher or student captures the essence of the idea.

○ Overview: the quick overview of the idea will help you select a new idea to read or re-find an idea you found useful on a previous flick-through.

○ Idea: the idea itself.

○ Hints and tips: additional teaching tips, suggestions for ways to take the idea further and bonus ideas are provided throughout.

Introduction

The ideas in this book are tried and tested from our time working together in the Beaumont School Music Department. But they are simply that – ideas. What works for one department may not work for another, but we are confident that each idea can be taken, adapted and tailored to suit you and your students.

Music is totally different from every other subject. Sure, lots of subjects will make this claim, but we really mean it. You cannot structure a music lesson like you would a 'normal' lesson, with students at desks scribbling away into exercise books. And you cannot assess music like you can other subjects; progress in music lessons happens in countless ways, directions and circumstances, at different speeds and at different times. When you are asked what your students are studying or to prove that your students are making progress, the answer is simple – play them some music. Language teachers are encouraged to use the target language, wherever possible, to help students internalise the cadence and structure of that language. All teachers are encouraged to consider their spelling, punctuation and grammar across subjects, to help students with their own English. It follows that the primary language of your classroom, your department, should be sound – it should be music.

Don't tell your students what a piece of music is all about, don't show them, let them hear it. Play your students what you want them to try, or to achieve. If they make a mistake, let them hear what it should (or could) sound like.

This entire book is written on this premise. Every idea, however practical, however brief, has behind it the guiding principle that music is everything in music education.

Tweet us on @daveguinane and @myhanhdoan for discussion on any of these ideas.

Physical warm-ups 1

"Performing and rehearsing is like sport: you need to warm up."

Whether you are with a KS3 class or your auditioning chamber choir, warm-ups should be thorough and fun. If you expect your students to give one hundred per cent, you must prepare them properly for it.

There are a lot of books out there which give plenty of ideas for warm-ups, but stick to the principles covered here and in Idea 2 and you will have covered the essentials. This idea covers the physical warm-ups.

Don't underestimate the value of and need for some basic stretches and movement. Making music (especially singing) is tiring if done properly, so make sure the right muscles have been warmed up:

○ Start with some basic breathing exercises to focus the students: breathe in, *Lesson 1.* hold and release for five seconds each. Focus on posture in particular, and controlling the release of breath – this will also diffuse any chatter and silliness.

○ Stretching: arms in the air meeting at the top, stretch and lean left and right. This will relax the body and get rid of any tension.

○ Diaphragm exercises: put your hands on your diaphragm and make sounds such as 'ft ft ft' and 'sss sss sss' feeling how the diaphragm expands and contracts.

○ Shoulder massage: If you want to add a bit of fun, get the students to stand in a line, one behind the other, and put their hands on each other's shoulders. Then ask them to give each other a gentle massage!

○ Face stretches: the best bit! Massage your cheeks, pretend you are chewing gum and make faces to exercise those muscles, e.g. screwed up face ('cat's bottom') and open mouth ('scared rabbit').

Top tip

Make sure you model these warm-ups yourself. The students will be much more willing to relax if they know you are prepared to do the same.

2 Vocal warm-ups

"Can't we just start singing?"

As well as your body needing to be physically ready, your vocal chords need good preparation too. This is also a great opportunity to tailor your warm-ups to your class's or choir's needs.

The warm-ups below merely scratch the surface of what you can do in lessons and rehearsals. You will have your own set of warm-ups, but don't forget to keep refreshing them too.

○ **Tongue twisters:** these are a good transition into vocal warm-ups. We all have our favourites but, if you're stuck, try 'red lorry, yellow lorry' or 'copper-bottomed coffee pot' – both sung to a scale.

○ **Warm-up songs:** there's nothing like a song to get the students going, as well as generally warm them up. There are plenty of great resources to choose from. *Voiceworks 1* and *Voiceworks 2* (OUP) and *Musical Futures* (**musicalfutures.org**) are two of the many available at the time of writing.

○ **Singing a scale by gradually building it up from the tonic:** '1, 1-2-1, 1-2-3-2-1' and so on. Doing this all the way through to 8 works well. Then ask students to miss out (and leave a gap) certain degrees of the scale when singing it again. This will make them focus and concentrate.

○ **Improving weak areas:** if your choir has a specific area for development, such as poor consonants or tuning, then find warm-ups which will improve these skills, for example exercises using *sol fa*, or singing triads and moving up and down in semitones.

Taking it further...

If you have students who sing and play outside school to a good standard, stretch them by asking them to prepare their own warm-ups which focus on specific skills.

Singing in lessons 3

"Everyone can sing."

Every student can get something out of singing, no matter what kind of sound comes out. If you sing from the moment students arrive in Year 7, you will establish your expectation that everyone sings in lessons at all ages.

Here are some useful tips for singing in lessons:

○ **Lead by example:** If you have inhibitions about singing, your students will too. There's no polite way to say it, but you need to get over it, open your mouth, and sing! Your students will not judge you on the quality of your sound, and the more you sing, the better you will get.

○ **Start as you mean to go on:** Singing is a great leveller and there is nothing better than starting Year 7 with a class or group singing project to bring the students out of their shells, and allow you to hear their voices in a non-threatening way. Fun warm-ups and starting with call and response will instil confidence in you and your students. There are plenty of resources available on the internet, e.g. the *Musical Futures* website noted in Idea 2.

○ **Don't isolate singing:** Once you have established a positive culture of singing, make sure it is part of your scheme of work all the way through to A-level. Warm-ups related to your topic will get lessons off to a musical start, and vocalisations of instrumental ideas (e.g. riffs) will help students internalise musical ideas. There's not much the students can't sing!

Top tip

When the going gets tough, don't give up. The boys may lose enthusiasm as they struggle in Years 8 and 9 when their voices start to drop. But, talk to them about the changes, and try to find music to suit their voices, e.g. vocalisations or beatboxing.

Taking it further...

Singing should be integral at GCSE and A-level. There are always suggested repertoires or set works that can be sung, and vocalised versions of others are always good fun. Singing helps students internalise, which is essential for A-level harmony. Bring the music to life by performing it, no matter how mad you think the idea is!

4 Engaging starters

"Think about musical, relevant, and effective lesson starters."

Get creative with the way you start your music lessons to ensure your students are engaged right from the beginning!

Teachers often rely on the same clapping games or vocal warm-ups to fill the first five minutes of lessons, and tick that 'starter' box. Yet the start of the lesson could be so much more…

Here are some considerations when planning the start of your lessons:

○ Have music playing as students enter: Students then have no doubt that they are entering a music classroom, and that the primary language of the lesson is music. Play professional recordings, YouTube videos, or their work from previous lessons. If suitable, have some questions on the board for either quiet discussion or private thought.

○ Singing starters: Please sing, as often as you can, but make it relevant to the material covered in the lesson. Tongue twisters and other warm-ups (see Idea 2) might be appropriate if the rest of the lesson is singing and improving vocal skills. If your lesson is primarily instrumental or computer-based, singing can help students internalise the music they are covering. For example, if you are improvising in a blues style, sing some typical blues phrases; if you are performing a tango piece, sing the tune to scat syllables, and play with dynamics and articulation. Students then instantly see the possibilities of an exciting performance, without having the barrier of their developing technical instrumental skills.

Taking it further...

Have music playing at other times as well, e.g. when students come in for rehearsals, assembly or form group – and likewise if you run a meeting for members of staff. It is a great way to show others your musical personality, and your passion for your subject.

○ Rhythm game starters: There are countless rhythm games that could be used as starter activities, but again consider relevance. A tricky syncopated rhythm in a performance is the perfect thing to clap, stamp or sing at the start of a lesson, but ensure students make the link between this activity and the music that forms the 'core' of the lesson.

○ Starter to think about progression: Give students time to consider where they are with their work, and how they are going to improve it this week. Use feedback, recordings and 'The A3 Sheet' (see Idea 24) to help you with this.

○ Play for the students: Live performance is special, in any form. Improvise something based on the material covered in lessons; a fantasia on a KS3 tango, or a simple blues will engage students. It doesn't even have to be that good; most students are a very appreciative audience!

○ Be careful with worksheets: Avoid worksheets that go over key terms, or listening activities that just require students to fill in boxes. Time is precious in music lessons, so ask yourself if the first thing students do in your lesson is just there to fill time, or if it is genuinely musical.

Bonus idea

You could lose the 'starter' altogether. If you have the right class, experiment with sending students into groups straight away. You might bring them back after a while, once they have revisited what they were doing in the previous lesson. You could introduce new ideas at this point.

5 How to end a lesson

"Stop, take stock, and look forward."

Have an activity up your sleeve to round off your lesson or help students consolidate what they have learnt – whether you have time for it or not!

Let's face it, most plenaries involve running around like a headless chicken, packing away percussion, and trying to tidy up before the next lesson. If the learning in the main part of the lesson is going well, it is all too easy to allow students that little bit longer to make progress, and end up with a mad rush at the end. There isn't anything wrong with this; if your judgement is that extra time doing practical is more important than a 'tacked-on' plenary, go for it. There are, however, a number of useful things you can do at the end of your lesson to cement learning or lay the groundwork for future learning.

Listen to performances

❍ Though the 'assessment lesson' is generally a bad idea (putting product above process, and ultimately progress), sharing work is almost always a good thing.

❍ Don't always hear the best group; it can be demoralising for others, and if it is too perfect, where is the opportunity for further progress?

❍ Go for quality over quantity; better to hear one group and have a good discussion about where they are, and where they could go next, than hear four groups and not say anything about the music.

❍ Workshopping; leave time to isolate sections of a performance. Have individuals play their ideas, and ask students to explore ideas there and then.

❍ Record it all!

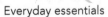

Planning

○ Give students time, whether alone, or in their groups or pairs, to plan ahead. What do they need to remember? What do they need to do to make their piece better? They can jot down a few words or phrases, or record a short audio clip on a phone or department device.

Discussion

○ Go over key musical concepts. How well do students understand them? Do they have any questions? What was the most difficult part of the task? (This should inform *your* planning for the next lesson.)

○ As well as asking a group's 'audience' for 'two stars and a wish', ask the performers themselves; their perspective is important.

Videos and music

○ Videos and music are often used to 'hook' students in at the start of a lesson and create a buzz about the music you are about to create. Why not do the same at the end? Shouldn't your students leave your classroom humming a tune, talking about something they have seen or heard and buzzing about music?

Bonus idea

Why wait until the end of the lesson to share a group's work, or discuss a musical concept. Have a mini-plenary in the middle of the lesson; there are fewer time constraints, and it allows students time to act on feedback, or what they have heard.

6 Working with peers

"The music classroom is the perfect setting for implementing a variety of group, paired and solo work."

Space and time will often constrain what is possible, but striking a balance between the three approaches – group, pairs and solo – will engage your students, especially if you often change around pairs and groupings.

Some topics lend themselves well to group work, whereas students might make better progress in other topics if they work by themselves. How will you decide? Here are some suggestions for group, paired and solo work for you to consider:

Group work

This provides a great opportunity for students to take on roles in a musical performance. It is important that each student makes a significant contribution to the rehearsal or composition process and performance.

○ Riffs and hooks performances or compositions can be a great opportunity for groups of four or five students to create a composition that includes chords, one or two riffs, a bassline and melody.

○ Four-chords compositions and performances are also ideal for group work. Start with everyone playing the chords and bassline, and add in vocals and backing harmonies when ready. The students love this one and if they are put in the right groups, the results can be very exciting.

○ From the start of Year 7, allocate your students into groups for singing. This will set them up for the next three years and beyond. Whether it be African chant or pop arrangements, the social skills required to make this a success (especially when

| Top tip |

Mix and match the approaches to get the balance right. If you feel a project has become stale, change the groupings. Choose your groups and pairings wisely but also include some free choice. Whilst this can often give rise to unsuitable combinations (as well as some excellent ones), it also conveys an element of willingness on your part.

the students don't know each other at the start of Year 7) are key to a flourishing music classroom.

Paired work

Where there is not enough room for group work, paired work can often be the solution.

◗ Using keyboards is an ideal occasion for paired work. The important thing is to ensure that the two students in each pair swap roles regularly so that it isn't only one student who improvises or plays the melodies while the other plays single-fingered chords for a whole unit.

◗ Improvising is another great skill to develop in pairs. Students can easily lose heart working individually on this, whereas when working in pairs they can keep each other in check with which notes to use. If needed, they can come up with a short melody together first, to familiarise themselves with the notes. This will will give them the confidence to start improvising.

Solo work

It is very rare in the music classroom for genuine solo work to be a frequent occurrence, mainly due to constraints of time and space. However, consider the following situations which can offer opportunities for solo work:

◗ After students have 'prepared' improvisations, give them an opportunity to improvise individually in front of the class.

◗ Solo spots in classroom singing give an opportunity for you (and the rest of the class) to hear individual voices.

Taking it further...

Take a risk and use an online student selector to randomise pair or group selection. There are plenty you can use, but Triptico does this very well, and contains plenty of other teaching tools and resources (**tripticoplus.com**).

7 Gifted students

"What will you do for my son who is already Grade 6?"

A gifted student is someone who performs to a very high standard, or has a natural sense of musicianship or a 'good ear'. Stretching these students in the music classroom along with everyone else can be difficult.

Top tip

At KS4 and KS5, give more able students the more difficult parts in class performances and ask them to lead rehearsals and group work. Set them wider listening tasks to broaden their horizons and, of course, target them with higher-level questioning.

Taking it further...

Don't forget that, whilst many of your gifted students may have excellent performing skills, you will come across students who have little performing experience but will have a good ear for improvisation and demonstrate superb musicianship. As well as pushing them in class, encourage them to join extra-curricular groups to gain more performing experience.

An important point to remember in the music classroom is that there is no end point to progress. There is always something that can be refined and improved at every level. Here are some ideas:

○ Invite your gifted students to bring in their instruments to play in class performances and compositions. If they play a transposing instrument, show them how to transpose their music or encourage them to play by ear.

○ If a student is a competent keyboard player, can he or she play more complex parts, e.g. a chordal accompaniment that the teacher might normally play?

○ Improvising is often a good leveller in the KS3 classroom; just because someone is good at the clarinet, it doesn't mean they have developed their improvising skills. Encourage the students to shape and extend their improvisations, as well as provide more complex accompaniments. The same goes for compositions.

○ Giving gifted students the role of 'teacher' is another way of challenging them. Organising group work and coordinating group compositions will always challenge students, particularly when you have grouped them according to mixed ability.

A sense of pulse 8

"How can I help my students to find their internal metronome?"

A sense of pulse is an important skill a musician needs in order to develop. As a secondary music teacher, your best-laid plans can crumble very quickly if students are not able to keep in time. Help students develop their sense of pulse so they can benefit from the musical opportunities you provide.

How can you help your students develop a sense of pulse? Try these ideas:

● Vocalise the beat: Students benefit from saying '1, 2, 3, 4' as they play, to help them stay in time. Over time they can start to accent different beats with their voice, further developing their musicality in performance.

● Get students to move! Stamping, swaying, raising their arms, encourage whatever movement is appropriate for the music you are covering. Students naturally nod their heads to music they know, so encourage them to do the same with new music they encounter.

● Concentration: Students need to stay 'in the moment' to stay in time. To start with, choose something for students to play that engages them. Demonstrate what it should sound like and make sure they are listening as you play. As you rehearse students, or work with groups, find the moment their concentration drops (and the piece nose-dives) and focus on avoiding that.

Top tip

Use music they know. Students will find it easier to engage with the pulse if they are already familiar with other musical aspects. Include beatboxing (sometimes). Students often perform more naturally in time when beatboxing, as the music is so engaging. Clapping games and counting only gets you so far. Make sure you are applying concepts of rhythm and pulse to real music.

Taking it further...

Work hard on developing a student's sense of pulse. Alongside this, remember to work equally hard on developing other musical skills, such as their creativity, sense of pitch, etc.

9 Students with SEND

"Maximise the musical experience for every child."

Every child, no matter who they are, can access, or benefit from music, with careful consideration as to how it is delivered to them.

Here are some tips or strategies for working with students with SEND, who may find it harder to progress and stay engaged. Remember that every child is different.

● Simplify parts, especially for students with physical disabilities, so that everyone has a part they can access (but which still challenges them) and can experience the joy of a successful group performance or composition.

● Provide some structure for students with conditions like autism, without reducing the spontaneity and vibrancy of your music lessons. Students who struggle with disruption will be more comfortable with an outline of what they are going to do, and when.

● Focus on what students can do and ensure that musical progress is the core aim in every activity you plan. If a student with SEND is at their most creative when working alone, or when using ICT, it is a good idea to make this a bigger part of their individual curriculum. However, don't assume they will work better alone or with ICT.

● Be guided about an individual's needs from colleagues, but remember that often students who struggle to engage in other subjects can be totally different in a music classroom. Ensure your interventions and differentiation help their musical progress, and not just their behaviour.

Musical Futures 10

"Its pedagogy has transformed many music departments across the country."

Musical Futures started out in 2003 as an action research programme, designed to find new and innovative ways of engaging young people in meaningful and sustainable musical activities. It is widely used in education today, both here and abroad.

Musical Futures (musicalfutures.org) consists of two approaches, which have been tried and tested by classroom teachers. The programme focuses on non-formal teaching and informal learning.

Since its inception, *Musical Futures* has evolved and changed with the times. Originally opening our eyes to 'informal learning', it has become a central resource for every music teacher. If you are stuck for ideas at KS3, or you have moved into a department in which student engagement is an issue, these are some of the things it can offer you:

● 'Find your voice' – an approach which develops students' confidence and mastery of their voice.

● 'Just play' – a skills-based approach, with music-making at the heart of KS3 teaching.

● A wealth of resources.

● Practical strategies and suggestions for composing at KS3 and 4.

As well as the ideas listed above, workshops are run throughout the country. You can also go on one of their training course. You will find that their passion for music education is nothing but infectious.

Bonus idea

Why not head along to MufuChat on Twitter (#mufuchat) which is held every Wednesday night at 8.30pm (UK time). It gives you an opportunity to discuss issues facing music educators with other colleagues on Twitter. It's a great way to build an online network for yourself, especially if you are in a solo or small department.

11 Worksheets (and cover work)

"Is it OK to use worksheets in music lessons?"

With the best will in the world, sometimes you need to give out bits of paper in music lessons. Similarly, for whatever reason, sometimes you aren't going to be there, and will need to set cover.

There are thousands of pre-made resources out there; entire books and websites dedicated to A4 sheets of paper that are 'ideal' for music lessons. They can be a huge time-saver (especially when setting cover) but you do need to think carefully about whether worksheets are really enhancing the musical learning of your pupils. Here are some useful tips to help you.

Worksheets – less is more

Think about whether you could reduce the number of worksheets you use in KS3 (see also Idea 24). Ask yourself:

⊙ Is this worksheet full of facts about a particular style of music? Could I teach these through performance and/or composition, deepening students' understanding of certain musical features?

⊙ Is this worksheet a listening task? If the questions promote musical learning, could I do this listening activity in a more engaging fashion? (See Idea 44).

⊙ Is this a horrible theory worksheet I am just giving out to use up time? If yes, bin it. Now!

For KS4 and KS5, when exam preparation looms, more content needs to be put on paper. Consider the following:

○ Provide a list of headings, with just keywords and bar numbers, and ask students to fill in the rest (with your help). The more active they are, the better the learning. A list of musical features is a waste of time.

○ Leave space on the worksheet for students to add annotations, and make sure you use musical examples (i.e. notation) as well as words.

○ Leave space for reflection and planning. A composer's jotter can help students order (or just remember) their ideas.

Cover

Teaching might be the only profession where phoning in sick creates more work than just muddling through the day feeling terrible. Don't feel guilty about setting cover, but consider the following:

○ If you are ill, a worksheet printed off from the internet is fine (e.g. from a subscription website such as **musicalcontexts.co.uk**). Try and make it related to the work you are doing, but don't beat yourself up if musical learning is not perfect.

○ If you have good cover supervisors, try and create a culture in which students can get on with practical work. This isn't easy; it is about ensuring students value music, respect the subject and department, and can be trusted in your absence. If that is the case, you can set cover that says: 'Students are doing X. Let them get on with it, and if you fancy it, hear some performances at the end' – and students will actually be *making music* in your absence.

Taking it further...

Can you 'flip' your learning (see also Idea 12)? Rather than spending valuable lesson time on key terms, or listening activities, can you set this work as homework? Similarly, if you have homework you are planning to set, and suddenly find yourself at home and unwell, set that homework for your cover lesson.

Bonus idea

If you have access to technology in your classroom, or to students' devices, use them. Ask students to do some research in your absence, or write about and analyse music they have already produced. (It is useful to have a bank of recordings ready and available.)

12 Making homework relevant

"But SLT says it's school policy to set homework at Key Stage 3..."

The homework issue has several layers. You need to balance accommodating the whole school homework policy whilst still setting meaningful and valuable homework.

Homework for KS4 and KS5 is usually straightforward to set; there is always plenty of practice the students could be doing, as well as preparatory listening, essay plans, harmony exercises, etc. At KS3, however, the debate is a hot one. How many times do you see your KS3 classes and for how long? Do you think you can set homework that contributes to musical progress for all of your classes, and manage the marking? If you do set homework at KS3, then consider the following:

❍ Flip your learning: Get students to do at home some of the task you might normally do at school, such as listening to the core work. If you have a blog or Twitter, share ideas and ask students to tweet back, if appropriate.

❍ Virtual learning environment: If you have a VLE (you could use Edmodo or something similar if not), upload listening files or post links and worksheets.

❍ Worksheets: If you choose to set a worksheet, try to avoid setting work that is not relevant to your current unit of study or is onerous to mark. Don't go creating more work for yourself. And avoid setting worksheets with no follow-up (such as notation worksheets or research into composers).

❍ A listening log: This always works well and provides a good discussion point at the start of the next lesson.

❍ Takeaway homework: Give students options to select from each week.

Taking it further...

Create a display of homework which really demonstrates students' independent learning skills. It could be listening logs with QR codes to some of the pieces, or research into a style, again with some links to students' work.

Talking to parents **13**

"What to say without putting your foot in it."

There are so many aspects of music that need covering in a parent consultation that you can often end up saying a lot but conveying nothing! Consider the key things you want to put across to the student's parents. It won't be the same for every student, so don't make it the same.

Start with a question to bring the student and parents into the conversation. No one likes a monologue, and you can't sustain that approach all night! If the student thinks they are doing OK, you can agree and say something positive.

If conversation doesn't open up naturally, then say something about performing, listening and composing. Give a strength and some areas for development. Continue to ask the student open-ended questions in order to maintain conversation flow: 'How do you feel about…?'

If you think you are going to have a difficult conversation, make sure you get some support. Ask your line manager or member of the leadership team to come to the consultation or simply hover close by in case you run into any difficulties. If there is a problem, make sure you can suggest a solution and offer your support. If there is a bigger issue, you may have to finish the meeting and meet the parents at a different time.

Finally, don't forget that this is also the perfect time to grab a student who you think should be attending an extra-curricular group!

Top tip

It is entirely up to you whether you mention levels at KS3 or not. Some parents might ask. If the question of levels arises, make sure you explain that musical progress is not linear (maybe this is the point where a monologue is more appropriate). At GCSE and A-level, it becomes more appropriate to discuss target grades/potential grades, particularly if you are concerned about a student's progress.

Taking it further...

Set up a laptop with some headphones and have a bank of student performances ready for parents to listen to. This will give them the best idea of what goes on in the classroom.

14 Planning lessons

"Failing to plan is planning to fail."

There really is only one way to teach music: musically. This is easier said than done. Music lessons can easily descend into chaos, and this is often due to poor planning.

Plan your lessons carefully to maximise the musical experience for your students:

○ **Plan the students' entry:** Having music playing on arrival is essential: it ensures students know they are entering a musical space.

○ **Plan the transitions in your lesson:** Work out how you are going to get students into groups/pairs, and how you are going to get them back again.

○ **Plan time for sharing, or workshopping students' ideas:** Ensure students have time to act upon any feedback given.

○ **Plan the end of the lesson:** Make time for packing up, and the activity you intend for the end of the lesson. Don't let students leave the classroom in a rush. It will affect their learning, and you'll regret it when your room is a tip.

○ **Allow as much time as possible for practical music-making:** If students need re-focussing, bring them back together to hear some work, or model a more advanced concept, and then send them back to making music.

○ **Keep it simple:** Lots of music lessons might seem very similar to one another, but that doesn't matter.

A typical music lesson plan

Students enter, music is playing.
Students hear the previous week's work.
A new concept is introduced, or another is reinforced. This is done through practical modelling.
Students are given time to apply these musical concepts to their practical work. The teacher circulates, makes recordings and gives musical feedback.
A group's work is heard. Students and teacher give feedback.
Students are given more time to progress with their practical work. The teacher circulates, makes recordings and gives musical feedback.
The work of more groups is heard. Feedback is given.
Students plan how they will progress further in the next lesson.

Top tip

Trust yourself. As music teachers, the majority of our time is spent rotating round groups or pairs, and giving musical feedback. No amount of non-musical activities, however 'showy', can replace this.

Taking it further...

GCSE and A-level lessons need to be as practical as those at KS3. Performing set works, or demonstrating musical concepts through singing or playing, are objectively the best ways to help students progress. Ensure any teacher-led lessons are heavily punctuated with opportunities to perform or compose, however brief.

15 Musical feedback

"Music is the most powerful language in the music classroom."

In your lessons, you are asking your students to make music by using and improving their performing, composing and listening skills. It stands to reason therefore that, when giving feedback, musical feedback is the most powerful way to help students improve.

How can you effectively give musical feedback in the music classroom?

❍ Play along: Students often struggle with the rhythm once they have mastered the notes when reading notation. Play their part with them; it will improve their playing instantly.

❍ Improvise: Improvise over the top of a student's chord sequence or piece based around riffs, to show them where they could take their piece next. Encourage the students to do the same. Use question and answer phrases to help them. The best melodies are created when students have the confidence to improvise and try new things.

❍ Play, don't say: Instead of saying 'Perhaps you could add an A minor chord here', play it and let them hear it.

❍ Vocalise rests and harmonic changes: Students often struggle to hear when chords should change, and to keep their internal metronome going whilst playing (see Idea 8). Asking them to vocalise beats and chord changes, counting out loud and calling out the names of chords, will help them make progress.

❍ Make recordings available: Even if you model a piece at the beginning of a lesson, students may well have forgotten how it is supposed to sound by the time they get started. Have recordings accessible in the cloud so students can listen to them while working in groups.

Written/verbal feedback **16**

"How can I put musical progression into words?"

Although we have emphasised the importance of musical feedback in Idea 15, many schools will require written feedback in some form. Written and/or verbal feedback does complement musical feedback, as long as you do it properly.

Here are some ways to approach written and verbal feedback:

○ **Don't say something that doesn't mean anything:** The phrase 'play more musically' is of no use to a student looking at what he or she did two weeks previously.

○ **Be specific:** Giving feedback such as, 'Focus on staying in time with your group' is great, especially if it is accompanied by a musical demonstration of what this sounds like (maybe tacked on to the end of the group's last recording?).

○ **Praise as well as target:** Students need to know what they are doing well, so they can build on it and progress further. For example, 'Excellent use of ostinato. Now try and harmonise this using these chords.'

○ **Annotate the resources the students are using:** If the resources contain all musical material, success criteria and space for student notes, make sure they also contain a spot for teacher feedback. Draw arrows to things students might like to include, or are using really well. Words should always link as closely as possible to music.

Top tip

Use a single pen colour when annotating or writing on students' work, and date your comments. That way inspectors, students and you can easily see what feedback you gave and if students have acted on it.

Bonus idea

Ask students to comment on work. The ability to speak and comment perceptively about music they hear is a valuable skill for our budding musicians; they should be given the opportunity to demonstrate this skill, and develop it.

17 Recordings

"Recordings are an excellent way to demonstrate progress over time."

Demonstrating progress over time is a dreaded Ofsted phrase. Of course progress is what we all want for our students, but it's the 'demonstrating' bit which can really get music teachers in a tizz.

If you are going to demonstrate any kind of progress, then it has to be musical. A progress tracker with multiple dates and colours may be a good way of giving evidence, but as we discuss in Idea 18, the students' work exists in sound, so surely the best evidence and way of tracking progress is in the same format?

Recording students regularly gives them an opportunity to reflect on their work and improve it. It also helps students who are unable to notate ideas very quickly make sense of the brief notes they have made on paper.

How often should you record students?

Because all of your topics will focus on different skills, taking only one recording at the end of a unit is not particularly useful. Feedback such as, 'Try to compose your melody using the notes from the chords' is not much help at the end of a topic when your next topic is samba drumming!

Consider making recordings more frequently during the course of a topic. You can play them back to the students as examples of work each week and, importantly, if you record different students each week, it won't be as crucial if they miss the final performance lesson.

Top tip

Choose your recording device wisely. Most phones have a useful 'voice memo' or recording app that makes recording easy. If you are happy to use your phone in lessons, consider it. Alternatively, use a department device (e.g. tablet). Portable hand-held recorders offer improved audio quality, but getting the tracks organised can be a pain – although some will synch with your computer.

Feedback at the end 18 of recordings

"Where can I find the feedback you gave us for our group's composition?"

Why do we give feedback in music? We do it so our students' work gets better, and to improve the quality of their musical outcomes. We do it to give their performances more accuracy or nuance, or to allow their compositions to explore more complex ideas or structures. It should not be Ofsted-driven.

Ofsted are right; the feedback we give should relate to a student's musical development over time, and someone coming into our lessons should be able to see (actually, hear) this.

The work students produce is music, and exists as sound. Your feedback should be, at least in part, musical, and therefore also exist as sound.

As discussed in Idea 17, a collection of recordings, made over time, is undoubtedly the best way of tracking a student's musical progress. So, why not record your feedback at the end of a recording?

This idea is so simple you'll wonder why you didn't think of it before. Record yourself giving your feedback at the end of the recording. When a student returns to a project, they can listen to what they have done, as well as your feedback as to how to make it better and they don't have to waste time searching their folder of worksheets to find your written advice.

Top tip

Any form of feedback can be added to recordings: teacher feedback; peer assessment; self-assessment; teacher performance/ modelling; peer performance/ modelling. The options are limitless!

Taking it further...

Record whole workshops, or rehearsals, and make them available to your students. That way they can consolidate the feedback you give them ahead of their next musical experience.

19 Thinking about progression

"What does musical progression look like?"

Progression in music is complex. This idea provides a few tips that scratch the surface of progression and assessment in music, along with some more general thoughts.

Assessment and progression in music education is the subject of many books, seminars, papers and discussions, far beyond the scope of this book. Its complexity makes it a fascinating subject for study, but a real nightmare in everyday music lessons!

Progression in music is *not* linear. A student who performs well in a unit on the blues isn't then guaranteed to perform better in a following unit on ground bass. Bach would ace a unit on fugue, but might struggle with hip-hop or techno (actually, Bach would probably be amazing at both!).

Spirals

An alternative way of thinking about music progression involves spirals. Students improve their ability and make progress as they spend more time on a particular project. When something different comes along, they fall down the spiral and begin to make their way up again. The specific skills they improve (and how much they improve them) will be different depending on the music they are looking at. (See Martin Fautley's blog: **drfautley.wordpress.com**. Search for 'spiral curriculum'.)

Progress takes many forms

Is a good musician a performer? Or a creative composer? Is a good musician someone who really understands musical contexts and history? No two musicians are alike. You cannot expect all of your students to progress at the same rate across these different facets of being a musician; understanding this is key to understanding progression in music.

Provide for progress

How can we help students progress, if progress is so difficult to consider? We can think about 'providing for progress'; creating an environment in which every student can make exceptional progress *for themselves*. This is not easy, and involves the topics we cover, the feedback we give, the approaches we take – essentially, it is about *how* we teach music. (See Ben Sandbrook's blog: **bensandbrook.com/providing-for-progress**.)

Can do or can do musically?

Does it matter how many chord progression there are in a student's composition, or if they can play the most technically-demanding part in a performance? Or is it more important how *musically* a student can do something? Doing something, and doing it musically are two different things, and it is this latter musical progress we must strive for.

Top tip

There are few answers to the questions raised here, only a set of considerations and guidelines that should be part of your music lessons. It won't happen all the time, but as music teachers it is our duty to provide for, encourage, and record (yes) progress as best we can.

Bonus idea

Catch it when you can. Progress can happen at any moment. It is important to be involved with a student's musical learning every step of the way, not just when they perform at the end of a unit. It could be something they try in rehearsal that doesn't make it to the final piece, or a comment they make after the first run-through, that shows the musical progress they are making.

20 Assessing without levels

"Levels are no longer stipulated, so where do I start?"

Current guidelines in education do not stipulate that National Curriculum levels should be used to measure students' progress. We live in a brave new world, where we can choose any new system to ensure students make maximum progress in our lessons. But where do we start?

At the time of writing, many secondary schools are still using levels. The issue with using levels in music is that:

● they assume linear progress, which, as we have discussed in Idea 19, does not apply to progress in music

● they attribute very specific sub-levels (e.g. play with two hands instead of one); again, this doesn't reflect the nature of progression in music.

ISM National Curriculum for Music

An alternative starting point is an approach given in the ISM National Curriculum for Music document. This is an outstanding (and freely available) document that provides a framework for musical assessment at KS3. It is by no means a guide on how to assess Music at KS3 (no one will never know the perfect answer to that), more a planning aid to ensure you have planned for musical learning and progression.

Essentially, the assessment system involves breaking down the music you cover in your lessons into the skills, knowledge and understanding (with an emphasis on skills) that you feel are important for your learners. A three-point scale is suggested; 'not yet able to', 'able to', and 'exceeds'. How you define these is entirely up to you. Over time (a long time), you can build up a detailed picture of what your students can do musically, as well as the journey they have been on to get there.

Taking it further...

This idea only scratches the surface of assessing without levels. It is a huge subject, far beyond the scope of this book. For further reading, Martin Fautley's work on assessment has always proved to be a guiding light (e.g. *Assessment in Music Education*, OUP).

Assessing with levels 21 (no sub-levels)

"What is the difference between a 5b and a 5c?"

Ofsted has told us that levels are not necessary, as they cause a number of problems, particularly in music education. Yet many schools still insist on using levels. This idea provides some help for those still using the levels system.

Why do many schools still insist on using levels? Maybe it is because they can't find a better system (levels by another name), or because every subject using a different system would be too hard for parents/students/SLT to understand. If your school is using traditional 'levels', how can you make sure your assessment is still musical, and therefore valuable? Here are some ideas, which we hope will help:

○ Assessment criteria: Have assessment criteria that focus on skills, and how well students develop those skills, rather than 'things' they include in their performances or compositions (see Idea 20).

○ Best-fit levels: Use 'best-fit' levels, and ensure that the intricacies of what a student is doing, and how they are progressing, are explained elsewhere.

○ Avoid sub-levels: Please, please, please, try not to use sub-levels. They are meaningless. If you absolutely have to, think of a, b, and c as a mark of how often or how securely a student is meeting a particular criteria (like the 'not yet able to', 'able to' and 'exceeds' example noted in Idea 20).

○ Use the language of levels as little as possible: Give feedback on students' progress in as many other ways as possible (see Ideas 16–18). Be strong, and explain the limitations of numbers as indicators of a student's musical progress to parents and SLT if you are ever challenged about 'two sub-levels of progress' per term.

○ Don't use them as targets with the students: Don't say to students, 'To get to the next level you need to…'; just make sure students know what to focus on to get *better*.

> **Top tip**
>
> Your feedback (musical or otherwise) is the most important thing when trying to ensure that students know where they are, where they are going, and how to get there.

22 Tracking non-linear progress

"The students need to know what they have achieved and how they will get better."

It's time to take those tracking sheets and turn them into something which is useful for you and your students, as opposed to fulfilling a one-size-fits-all school assessment policy.

Keep it simple and manageable

Wherever you are in the post-levels brave new world, try and keep your system simple. What will the students have to fill in in their folders? Will it be a list of general level descriptors that they will have ticked off over the course of a project or will it be just one number (and letter? – please, no!)? Whatever you do, it needs to be simple and manageable. Here are some ideas to help:

Tracking with no levels

Consider one A4 sheet of paper with a list of non-specific musical skills (performing, composing, listening) that will be covered during the course of the year with a 3–5 point scale of success (see Idea 20). Can you and/or the student date when a degree of skill has been achieved in the appropriate column, with a view to improving as many skills as possible by the end of the year?

How about using this data to produce a spider diagram of the student's musical progress? This is very simple to do using computer software. It provides a broad picture of the student's musical journey. It is very visual, and would be a great talking point at parent evenings! (See ISM National Curriculum for Music.)

Tracking with levels

If your school is still asking you to report in levels, then you need to consider how much detail to include in a tracker sheet. Will you award a level for each musical skill covered in a topic? Or will you award an overall level for the topic?

You could create a tracking sheet that includes a variety of sentences that act as 'level descriptors', grouped by level. Students can highlight or underline the phrases that they feel they have achieved from across the levels. You then award a 'best-fit' level that combines their assessment with your own.

Whatever you do, avoid the sub-level. If your school wants you to report with a sub-level, then by all means do so, but leave it off your tracking sheet and explain to the students why.

Written comments

Written comments on a tracker have very little worth, for either the teacher or the student. Give concise verbal feedback at the end of recordings (see Idea 18) and make it available to the students and anyone who wants evidence of your intervention. Idea 16 will give you some ideas if you have to write a comment.

Top tip

Use student-friendly language on your tracking sheets, and make sure it means something. Whilst the ability to 'expressively manipulate musical elements' is an essential skill for all musicians, it is intangible and difficult to put into words. Terms like 'compose using key features of the style' give students more to go on. Strike a balance between formal criteria and your intuition as to what is 'musical'.

Taking it further...

As with making recordings, completing a student's tracking sheet does not have to wait until the end of a project. When you are going around your groups during a lesson, pick up a few trackers each time and have some discussions (and record them!). You will ease your own workload and students will learn to see progress as something fluid.

23 The transition to KS3

"Students bring together a wealth of musical experiences."

On arrival at secondary school, the students' musical experiences will be hugely varied. Your job is to bring them together and to begin to mould the students into the individual musicians that they will become.

Before the students arrive

○ Offer workshops to some of your feeder schools. Go in with a small group and lead some singing, playing or both. Avoid just offering a concert; try and include joint performances by your students and the primary students. Every age group will benefit from this. (See Idea 71.)

○ Invite Year 6 students to the dress rehearsal of a concert or production. They will get to see what goes on in your department and will get excited about what they can join when they arrive. (See Idea 71.)

When the students arrive

○ Ask students to share their various musical experiences in the first lesson. Give them as many opportunities as possible to show you what they know, and make links with what they will learn with you.

○ Be clear about your expectations and set your standards high. Music is different and can be hard, but it will also be fun.

○ Make sure your first lesson is musical. Be engaging, and start with some singing. Be mega-enthusiastic, no matter what time of day and how many Year 7 lessons you have taught that day!

○ Think about how will you sift out your instrumentalists. Will you ask for a show of hands or provide written questionnaires or passports? Or will you let them surface when they are ready? When you are ready, encourage the students to bring their instruments into lessons so it becomes the norm.

Top tip

Above all, be passionate about your subject! Passion is infectious and key to getting your students involved. Also, encourage the Year 7s to attend your extra-curricular groups.

Bonus idea

If you really want your Year 7s to get off to an explosive start, plan them a concert. Teach them a set of fun, engaging songs in lessons. Add in some soloists and instrumentalists and you will have a winning concert.

Structuring a unit 24

"This idea has transformed my teaching!"

How many of the bits of paper flying around your KS3 classrooms actually contribute to the musical progress of your students? This idea uses one sheet of A3 paper and no more!

In a typical KS3 unit, students need to be exposed to a musical style, feature or element, then become accustomed to performing in that style (or using that musical feature or element). Then they can begin to explore, edit, select, change ideas and compose in that style (or using that musical feature or element). A simple plan for a unit would be:

❍ Listen to some pieces in the style (or using the musical feature or element).

❍ Perform in that style.

❍ Using the above two, compose some works in that style.

The A3 sheet

Make one double-sided A3 sheet for your unit containing:

❍ Space for the student's name or class.

❍ Space for notes (musical, verbal or pictorial).

❍ Success criteria (use levels if you want).

❍ Space for students to log what they have done in one lesson, and what they need to do in the next.

❍ The 'musical materials' required (definitions, riffs, chords, instructions, whatever they need to access the particular style, feature or element).

❍ Space for teacher feedback and dialogue. Make it colourful, space it out in an interesting way, and add pictures. You now have everything you need to allow students to make musical progress across a unit – and no paper has been wasted!

> **Top tip**
>
> Use these sheets in conjunction with a well-organised collection of recordings to show students' progress and musical achievements. This stripped down approach is valuable to you (in terms of marking and assessing), to inspectors and leaders (who may only pop in to your lessons for a short while), and most importantly to students (who can see what they have done, and what they need to do next).

25 Where to find resources

"Should I feel guilty about using someone else's resource?"

Save precious time by finding existing resources and tailoring them to your students' needs!

Below is a list of recommended places you can find editable resources to download and adapt for your students (correct at time of publication).

○ tes.co.uk: Teachers frequently upload their resources here. You need to register to be able to download the resources, which are free of charge. They can vary in quality. Basic PowerPoint presentations can be a good start, as well as a variety of approaches to composition, etc.

○ musicalcontexts.co.uk: Here you are expected to pay a one-off fee of £85 (correct at time of publication). You have access to a wealth of KS3 resources, including lesson plans, listening resources, worksheets, starters and plenaries. Resources don't stop at KS3 and many of the GCSE areas of study from all the main exam boards are covered too.

Top tip

You won't like every resource in each collection recommended in this idea, so don't use them all. Mix and match as you feel appropriate – it might not even be the same each year.

Taking it further...

If you're having a lovely time downloading all these resources and marvelling at them, consider uploading resources you have created too!

○ musicalfutures.org: As well as online resources, *Musical Futures* offers a printed resource pack to dip into whenever you need.

○ Teaching Music: The eBook: *Teaching Music: Practical Strategies for KS3* (Rhinegold) contains a wealth of ideas for KS3, containing videos, hyperlinks and downloadable resources. Cost £49.50.

○ mtrs.co.uk: The *Music Teacher's Resource Site* is dated but does contain some detailed schemes of work and lesson plans, which can be adapted for today's classroom. Resources are free so it's worth a look.

○ Social media: Don't underestimate the power of Twitter and Facebook. For example, search for KS3 Music on Facebook and you will find resources and online support at your fingertips. If you ask for a specific resource, someone will have it or point you in the right direction. And you will probably get it for free.

Notation 26

"Introducing notation is like opening a can of worms!"

Given the fact that students learn to read and write from a very young age, and yet many are still learning to do so by the time they get to secondary school, do students really need to learn to read music as well, in order to make music in the KS3 classroom?

We are certainly not suggesting that teaching notation should be abandoned at KS3, but notation should not be a barrier to music-making and musical progress. Discussions about notation will be valuable and useful, but don't forget your lessons should above all be musical.

○ Give students the opportunity to learn basic rhythms and rhythm combinations in Year 7. Rhythm grids with 'X' notation provide an excellent start for the beginners, many of whom will go on to convert those to crotchets and quavers.

○ Most Year 7 programmes of study will include a keyboard unit, which ties in beautifully with learning notes in the treble (and bass?) clef.

○ Combining rhythm and pitch will be an issue for many KS3 students. Teaching this in isolation will have limited success: students need to see and hear how rhythms and pitches work in context.

○ When you are presenting music to be used by the students, refer to pitch names and shapes, and rhythms and recurring patterns. Keep it in the students' minds, but don't allow it to stop them from performing and composing.

○ Go for a 'little and often' approach and your students will (hopefully) absorb more and more shapes and the sounds they represent.

Top tip

Always relate notation to sound. Pick out interesting sections or phrases that the students are playing, and demonstrate how the notes go up and down on the stave and how they sound when you play them.

27 Reggae

"I love teaching reggae. The music is infectious, and full of joy. It can teach students so much about music."

Reggae is harmonically accessible, melodically inventive and rhythmically challenging. An oldie but a goodie, it deserves its place in a KS3 music curriculum.

Taking it further...

Make cross-curricular links with other departments, such as geography or history, and time your teaching of this unit to coincide. Possible cross-curricular topics include drugs, the Rastafari movement, and other social issues related to reggae.

Bonus idea !

Reggae is a 'classic' style to teach at KS3 and there are a large number of resources already available online: countless transcriptions of reggae pieces, or ready-made PowerPoints. As long as you make the resources appropriate for your students, and they form part of a musical approach to teaching reggae, you can save time in your planning.

Use reggae to teach the following:

❍ Performing: Students can perform off-beat chords (a challenge for some), syncopated bass lines (a challenge for many), and melodic riffs (more accessible). Everyone can sing, some can sing and play, and everyone makes progress. Group pieces work really well, as well as whole-class performances, and any instrument can be involved.

❍ Composition: Using primary chords to create verses and choruses is a great way to teach harmony. Writing riffs, bass lines and melodies with different levels of scaffolding offers everyone an accessible entry to composition. Writing words is a great means of expression for many students.

❍ Listening and appraising: Reggae music has a fascinating history. It covers civil rights, social issues in Jamaica as well as the UK, and many of its most famous artists led fascinating lives.

❍ Music technology: Sequencing reggae is accessible, but can be differentiated easily for more able students. Recording live reggae performances and 'producing' them using various effects and mastering techniques will also help students make musical progress.

❍ Repertoire: As well as the 'classics', reggae's rhythms, lyrics and ideas still reign supreme in contemporary pop music, and as such it retains its relevance for young musicians.

Four chords

"My students were astounded by how many famous songs use the four chords!"

'Four chords' has become a classic KS3 topic, lending itself well to consolidating work on chords, especially if you want to introduce melody writing over the sequence.

For those of you who don't know, the four chords used by many pop artists over time are: I–V–vi–IV (or C–G–Am–F in the key of C). The group Axis of Awesome famously put many of these songs into a medley, which can be found on YouTube (watch it before deciding whether to use it purely for inspiration for yourself or to show the students, as there is the occasional inappropriate word).

Students love writing a melody or singing over the four chords sequence; it provides fantastic results quite easily.

O Performing: After the students have learnt the four chords (on guitar/ukulele or triads on the keyboard), explore single fingered chords, changing the styles as appropriate to the styles of songs. Students can play the chord sequence and sing songs over the top as well. The scope for vocal workshops is huge: improving students' work by improvising/trying out ideas alongside them will lead to some exciting results.

O Composition: With a chord sequence already made for them, students can learn about writing effective melodies over a chord sequence. Encourage students to start moving away from melodies based only on triads and guide your more experienced students through the use of dissonance in melody writing as well.

O Listening: As well as listening to a host of pop songs using this chord sequence, you can start to compare these songs with songs that do *not* use the four chords. Can the students hear the difference? Use the songs from the Axis of Awesome medley as a starting point. Students love listening to the songs segue into each other; what's not to love about the Beatles' *Let it Be* followed by Elton John's *Circle of Life*?!

Taking it further...

The four chords could become the basis of an inter-form/house competition in which students are required to perform a number of these songs as a mash-up or individually.

29 Contemporary classical music

"Sir, it just isn't music."

What is music? This is a question that has caused endless debate amongst musicians, musicologists, scholars and learned folk for hundreds of years. Why can't our young people wade in on this question?

Teaching a unit on contemporary classical music is hard, but worth trying. It encompasses minimalism, graphic scores, and other aspects of avant-garde music that occasionally pop up at KS3. But more importantly, there is an opportunity here to teach students that music, and more specifically composition, is not just notes on a page that get written down and played. The sometimes unknown, sometimes process-based aspects of contemporary composition can be a powerful lesson for young musicians.

Sample activities could include:

● A class performance of Terry Riley's *In C*. Actually, more than one performance would be good; that way students understand that the same piece doesn't necessarily sound the same for each performance.

● A lesson on phasing, perhaps based on Steve Reich's *Clapping music*. Students learn that whole pieces can be formed by applying a simple idea to a small unit of sound.

● A lesson on musical gesture, based on the works of Mark Rothko or Morton Feldman. Whole class or group improvisation works best here, and encourages students to express themselves through music, free from the constraints of tonal functional harmony, or the conventions of a musical genre.

Taking it further...

A unit on graphic scores is a classic at KS3, and can produce some very creative responses. Use real music; find examples in books such as *Notations* by John Cage, or *Notations 21* by Theresa Sauer. Many of the composers featured in the latter book are still alive, and still working. Find them on the internet, and send them your students' work. We have had some enthusiastic responses from composers after sending students' interpretations of their work, which has really engaged our classes.

Technology

This unit provides a fabulous opportunity to use technology. Try some of these ideas:

● The app *TonePad* (or similar) uses a pentatonic scale to create repetitive ideas. Give one student an iPod and an amp, and provide the rest of the group with the five notes used. The combination of electronic-device instruments and traditional instruments can create powerful results.

● Record some soundscape gestures on instruments, then import the files into Audacity (free downloadable recording software), and play with different ways of organising and changing these sounds. Link this with the work of Pierre Shaeffer and *musique concrète*.

● Minimalism and the idea of using loops in sequencers is always an engaging approach for students. However, it is important to ensure the learning is focused on music, and creating musical pieces that develop, rather than simply being a lesson on how to work the sequencer.

Debate

Challenge the students to argue whether or not what they hear is music. Challenge their assumptions about what music sounds like, and how it is composed.

Bonus idea

You may feel that a 'debate' on the definition of music is beyond the scope of your short, infrequent music lessons. Why not suggest the idea to your debating society or PSHCEE teacher? *'This house believes that John Cages' 4'33" is not a piece of music'* is a great topic for discussion.

30 The blues

"I woke up this morning... Time to teach some blues..."

The twelve-bar blues is a staple of KS3 music schemes of work, but can often result in a tired, pedestrian unit where students are marked on their ability to play the piano (boogie woogie bassline and pentatonic improvisation). It doesn't need to be this way!

Taking it further...

Instead of just playing the music of delta bluesmen when explaining the blues (because it is timeless and those guys knew how to play), engage your students by searching out the countless pieces in the pop, funk, soul, hip-hop and rock genres that also follow the twelve-bar pattern.

Bonus idea !

You may not be the most confident scat singer, but if you want students to leave their comfort zone and improvise, you need to be willing to do the same. Sing scat as a starter, main activity, or just while you circulate listening to students' work.

The twelve-bar blues can be a great unit if you think carefully about what students can learn during a series of lessons.

Harmonic change and harmonic progressions: Using something as simple as the auto-chords on a keyboard, students can gain an understanding of chord changes, and the idea of 'feeling' four, eight and twelve bars of music. If students say or sing the chord names when they change, their understanding of chord progressions will improve immensely.

Singing with expression: Anyone can come up with a blues song; the melody is usually the same for three sets of four bars and is easy to sing. The style lends itself to melodic inflections, call and response singing, and lots of vocal expression.

One or two-note improvisation: A convincing twelve-bar blues improvisation in C can be achieved using only the notes C, G and B flat. Get students to copy simple one-note phrases, then two notes, then three, and see their improvising improve.

Performing in a band: The few distinct elements to the blues (chords, bassline and melody) make it ideal for forming bands in your KS3 music classes. Students can add their own twist on a blues, such as heavy metal power chords, hip-hop beats or acoustic fingerpicking.

Western classical tradition 31

"Classical composers are boring!"

Your music curriculum should be broad, diverse and engaging. It is important that you cover the Western classical tradition with your students. But why is classical music so hard to teach?

It is your job to help students see the value of classical music. Help them learn to play it, and engage with the tradition. Tell them the stories behind the music, teach them about harmony, melody, texture, and how these things were shaped and changed by great composers. Bring out what is beautiful, powerful, shocking and empowering about classical music.

How can we engage students with the Western classical tradition?

The BBC's *Ten Pieces* initiative is an excellent example of an inspirational way to introduce Western classical tradition genres. The BBC model produced two films, one for primary and one for secondary students, that showcase the revolutionary and exciting stories behind great pieces. Presented by well-known faces, and accompanied by engaging images, these films do a lot to break down the barriers between young people and classical music. The idea behind *Ten Pieces* is that students come away from the film inspired to create art (in any form) based on one of these pieces. It has been a huge success. So, what can we learn from this? Here are some ideas:

● Use the stories behind either the creation of the music, or the stories told by the music itself, to engage students.

● Allow students to respond not only through music, but also through visual arts, technology or literature.

● They must *experience* this music, and not just listen to it. Show them videos, allow them to see it live, make it real and relevant.

Top tip

The *Ten Pieces* website features arrangements of the pieces, adapted for all abilities. Play this music with your students. Whether you use the BBC's repertoire, find or create your own, it is so important that students experience this great music first-hand.

Bonus idea

If you are struggling for a way in, try film scores. It is probably the main way in which the general public is exposed to orchestral music. Engage students with themes and sounds they know, and then take them to the source.

32 Composition workshops

"The composition workshop provided a space for the development of ideas."

Introduce this workshop idea for free composition. It allows students to experiment more, and to appreciate how much can be done with the smallest of ideas.

Top tip

It is important to model these ideas. You want students to play and improvise with total freedom, so you need to be doing it yourself. Many students will feel out of their comfort zone without sheet music or musical structures they are used to, and will need encouragement to move away from the familiar.

Taking it further...

If students respond well to this creative approach, invite them to present short ideas for their own compositions in this setting. A simple four-bar phrase can be given a new lease of life through the exploration of harmonisations, embellishments, rhythmic ideas or countermelodies.

For this workshop idea, students sit in a circle, with their instruments in front of them ready to explore musical ideas. Try the following:

○ **Exploring note clusters:** Ask the students each to pick a note, either from a chord or at random, and all play the chord created at an mp dynamic. Ask students to change their notes, listening to the effect on the chord. Conduct this at first, then ask students to simply listen to and react to each other.

○ **Over a drone:** Ask students to play short musical ideas of no more than three notes that punctuate the texture over a drone. Ask them to listen to what they hear and try to respond to each other's ideas. Gradually extend the length of each idea as students become more confident.

○ **Individual idea exploration:** If a student plays an interesting idea during the exploration, ask the rest of the class to work it out, then try it at different dynamics, with different articulation or embellishments. Try it as an ostinato, or create chords out of the notes played. Explore as many different permutations of a single idea as possible.

○ **Play with gesture:** Tell students to think only about the sounds their instrument can make (rather than the notes). Use conceptual art or dance as inspiration to help students play more freely.

Choosing an exam board

"Decisions, decisions, decisions."

Any music teacher should be involved in the discussion about which exam board is best for the department (create a fuss if you aren't).

There is no perfect exam board. You need to find a best fit for you, and the musicians you will take through the course. If you are in a position of choice, consider the following:

○ **Content:** Will the course content inspire your students, and will it inspire you?

○ **Transition:** Are the skills and knowledge required by the GCSE course covered in your KS3 schemes of work? Beyond basic musicianship, are there any overlapping musical styles or traditions that will give your students a head start?

○ **Your musicians:** Do your students all have private instrumental tuition, leaving you with more lesson time for the 'listening paper'? How are they going to compose? How much teaching of 'how to use sequencing/notation software' do you need to plan, before you start teaching the course? Will you specify that everyone goes down a certain route, or give complete freedom?

○ **The nitty gritty:** Will composition briefs help or hinder your students? Are the lengths of performances and compositions required comforting, or restricting? Are set works right for your students, or would they benefit from a broad exploration of musical styles? How well does the course suit students from 'non-traditional' backgrounds like world music, or beatboxing?

Top tip

Beware: browsing teaching forums will give you plenty of negative feedback and reasons not to choose a certain exam board. A bad set of results, or a harsh moderation in a colleague's school can put you right off. However, it is important to choose a board based on its content and approach to music, rather than on hearsay and horror stories.

Bonus idea

You have real choice. Don't be restricted by the 'big three' exam boards, and even by a traditional GCSE. Diplomas or BTECs might be better for your students. Explore every course and every exam board before making this important decision.

34 Nursery rhymes

"Nursery rhymes can be an excellent introduction to analysis."

Analysing music is a difficult skill. It requires knowledge of Western notation, a thorough understanding of the elements of music and a wide-ranging musical vocabulary. It takes time to develop, and careful planning. Nursery rhymes may well be the answer to these problems!

Here is a list of reasons why using nursery rhymes to teach basic analysis skills is a good idea.

○ They use primary chords. You can explain the harmonisation of diatonic melodies, imperfect and perfect cadences, and simple chord progressions, for example, using the three chords of *Twinkle Twinkle Little Star*.

○ Students can mark phrasing, identify melodies moving by steps and leaps, as well as repeated rhythmic ideas.

○ Those who struggle with notation know the tunes inside out, so they can relate the dots on the page to something they can hear.

○ Students can sing the sequences, repeated phrases and melodic devices instantly, and then annotate their scores accordingly.

○ You can experiment with a range of accompaniment styles, exploring texture, harmony and rhythm.

○ A colour-coded, annotated nursery rhyme is essentially a simplified version of what students need to do when they analyse music 'for real'.

National anthems 35

"Please stand for the national anthem of U2–BECKY–stan!"

When working on basic composition skills, it is essential that any material you use is accessible to the students. National anthems are great for this.

Try the following:

○ Step 1: Take a selection of different countries' national anthems! Apply the same principles of analysis to them as you did with the nursery rhymes (Idea 34). Look at the number of bars per phrase, which phrases are repeated, and what kinds of chords might be used to accompany the melody.

○ Step 2: Divide the class into groups of 3–4, ensuring a balance of instruments and musical experiences where possible. Ask them to write their own national anthem, using balanced phrases and primary chords as part of the accompaniment.

○ Step 3: Ask the students to make up the country's name, basing it on the name of one or more members of the group (see the quote above!) They could additionally write some lyrics, but this is not necessary.

○ Step 4: Each group records/performs their work, announcing it by saying: 'Please all rise for the national anthem of…!' in an official voice. The results are usually great. The simplicity of most actual national anthems means that when students come up with their simple balanced phrases and primary chords, they feel that their work is somehow comparable and that they have succeeded. Some groups will provide lyrics, often tongue in cheek and political (last year's *Saudi A-MAE-bia* made references to oil and women's rights!), but best of all, the students should have fun.

○ Step 5: Appraise the results with the class. What were the most successful national anthems? If yours didn't sound as effective as everyone else's, why not?

Top tip

This activity is probably best suited to the KS3–KS4 transition, and works well after Idea 34, Nursery rhymes. However, it is also a good one for your GCSE students if they are struggling to come up with composition ideas.

Taking it further...

Keep your recordings so that you have a growing collection to play for each subsequent year group. No two collections are ever the same.

36 The transition from KS4 to KS5

"They don't become professional musicians overnight."

Between Year 11 and sixth form, students often lose their uniforms, grow a few inches and possibly change their hair. But many teachers expect them to have changed the way they learn too. They begin teaching their Year 12 classes expecting lessons to flow like perfect seminars. The reality is often a disappointment: 16-year-olds out of uniform shuffling awkwardly, not really knowing what you are going on about, but too polite/scared to ask.

Here are a few tips for getting started with Year 12:

O Vocal warm-ups, rhythm games and starters: These are fun, and if you follow the advice in this book (see Ideas 1–4), they have musical relevance for your KS3 students. So, why not include them at KS5? Sing diminished arpeggios to start lessons, vocalise typical melodic shapes for a particular style of music; make the A-level material fun.

O Don't lose practical music-making: Perform set works, sing through chorales, get students to play or sing appoggiaturas, grace notes or whatever else they need to know. They might become solitary composers when you get down to the nitty-gritty, but practical workshops will help get ideas flowing in the first place.

◎ Go back to basics with theory, but don't make it dull: Many teachers gloss over theory at KS4, as quite frankly there are more important things to be getting on with, like making music. At KS5, particularly with A-levels, you can't really get away with it. Teach the basics, but apply the theory to popular works; analyse songs and pieces that engage the students. Get those who have a theory background to teach those who don't. (You will find many who are from a non-classical background have a solid understanding of chord progressions and harmony but they do not realise it; bring this out of them.)

◎ Don't expect students to analyse full scores from the off: It is a new skill, a hard skill that many in Year 13 will still struggle with. In Year 12, they probably don't know what they are looking for.

‣ Begin by asking students simple questions about a piece.

‣ Then sort basic facts into the musical elements, e.g. 'What is the chord in bar 3?'

‣ Students then need to relate musical features to style or context, e.g. 'What is interesting about this chord?'

‣ Students might then be able to find stylistic features of a style in a score.

‣ The next step is to try to get your students to realise that music gets interesting when composers and artists play with musical conventions. Ask students questions about the work, e.g. 'What is the cadence in bars 15-16? How is this different from what you might expect to see?' It takes lots of practice and encouragement.

Bonus idea

Students also need to know about context, composers' biographies, and other contextual factors in order to fully appreciate what they learn from musical analysis. This will take time and application.

Top tip

Students are often overwhelmed by a full orchestral score or a dense piano part. Write out parts of the music for them the old-fashioned way – it can make it much clearer. By writing out and annotating sections themselves, or sitting and playing through melodies at a piano, their understanding gradually improves.

37 Four-part harmony

"A chorale a week keeps the harmony doctor away!"

We firmly believe that in order to teach four-part harmony effectively, you should get your students to sing a chorale a week throughout the year. Consolidate this learning by playing The Chorale Game, and you will see your students' aural and four-part harmony skills develop.

It doesn't matter whether you make it to two, three or four parts, or simply sing each line through, any kind of singing is valuable for internalisation. Analysis can start with key signatures and progress through to melodic shapes and chord progressions.

Once your students have grasped the basics of four-part harmony, play *The Chorale Game* (see below). It will consolidate their understanding of four-part harmony and develop their aural skills (particularly useful for those preparing for dictation at A2).

The Chorale Game

○ **Preparation:** Before you start, divide the class into teams. Four per team is ideal, as is a spread of SATB, but obviously it depends on the size and make-up of your class.

○ Set up a keyboard with headphones (ideally a set of headphones per team).

○ Take a phrase (or two!) from a reasonably simple chorale (i.e. easy key, not too many passing notes). Label the SATB lines randomly as melody 1, melody 2, melody 3 and melody 4.

○ Step 1: Give the students the key and starting note of each of the melodies 1–4 (not necessarily at the correct register – you don't want the student to simply guess which part is which based on the register) and indicate any other points of note (for example, crotchet anacrusis, etc.).

○ Step 2: One student from each group 'fetches' the first melody from the keyboard. They are not allowed anything to write on. They put on their headphones and you play them the melody twice.

○ Step 3: The student returns to his or her group and sings as much of the melody as they can remember. The others try and write it down.

○ Step 4: The next student then goes to the keyboard for either the same melody or the next melody, depending on how much they have been able to write down. Again, play it twice only.

Repeat steps 3 and 4 as many times as it takes for the teams to get all the melodies. Make sure *everyone* takes a turn fetching the melody from the keyboard.

Once the group has all four melodies written down, they then need to decide which melody is soprano, alto, tenor, and bass. The first group to write out the chorale and sing as many parts as they can (together) are the winners.

As an extension, the winning group could do some analysis of chords at the cadences, and justify why they think each melody belongs to each voice part.

Top tip

The memorising aspect of this game is a good way of encouraging students to try to memorise a whole phrase, not just note by note. It also encourages them to assess how they try to memorise melodies, and how effective they are. Ban the use of the keyboard until things are getting a little desperate or you are running out of time!

Taking it further...

Record the voice parts on different instruments so that students get used to listening to a variety of timbres, not just the clear percussive sound of the piano part.

38 Teaching set works

"Bin the summary worksheet."

Set works appear in several exam boards specifications, and even when they don't, looking in detail at a specific work is a great way to give students an in-depth understanding of a style, genre or tradition.

Here are some thoughts on teaching set works at KS4 or KS5:

O Perform set works: Take the time to find, or create, arrangements of set works that your classes can perform. There is no better way of exploring music than by performing it. Even if you play the chords and the whole class sing the melody line, or you simplify the music to just chords and a bassline, any performance is better than none.

O Don't produce a summary worksheet: Students gloss over it, then forget about it.

O Get students to analyse the piece themselves: For example, under a sub-heading 'texture', give students some bar numbers or sections and ask them to comment on what is interesting about texture in each of those places. Then discuss (don't just tell them) the key musical features of what they have found.

O Make sure they understand the context: Students need a list of features you might *expect* to find in a piece before they can analyse the revolutionary/unconventional aspects of it. Particularly at KS5, students need to understand *why* a piece has been chosen as a set work. This involves lots of listening around the piece, and performing other pieces in the same style.

O Ask students to produce a summary worksheet: The summary worksheet is fantastic for revision. Create a lesson, or series of lessons, and get the students to do most of the work. Guide them, help them, just don't tell them *all* the answers; their understanding will be greater if they put in the legwork.

Taking it further...

Share your arrangements online. If everyone did this, eventually there would be a significant repository of set work arrangements, helping teachers struggling with workload.

Bonus idea

Analysis is a skill that needs to be practised. Too many teachers assume that students can look at music and see what *they* see. For tips on teaching this skill, see Ideas 34 and 36.

"It's not just a list of key features!"

Many courses require in-depth knowledge and understanding of areas of study, either alongside, or instead of, specific set works.

Here are some things to bear in mind when teaching areas of study:

Dance, perform, sing and play

Sing common melodic ideas, play common rhythmic patterns, and dance if the style allows it! Perform actual pieces from that style, 'grooves' that you might find in that style, or students' compositions based on a particular area of study.

Use mini set works

Find a piece that includes most features from that style and study it as a mini set work. Get students to annotate the score in detail (after having performed the work, of course). This approach also helps when you are looking for possible repertoire to perform.

Listing musical features musically

At some point, you need to explain and list musical features, and students will need to copy them down or file a photocopy. However, before that, ask students to offer the explanations themselves. Give groups of students a number of key musical terms, and ask them to prepare a *musical* explanation, where they *show* students what that term sounds like. It can be isolated and performed on their instruments, or highlighted in context by playing an example piece (or ideally, both).

Taking it further...

Ask students to curate a week of wider listening based on an area of study, or prepare a playlist for your bedtime listening (see Idea 66). Ask them also to find the audio for your mini set works.

Bonus idea

Musical styles don't exist in a vacuum. All music is related. Ask students to draw out the key similarities and differences between related (or unrelated) areas of study. They could use Venn diagrams or comparison tables to formulate their thoughts.

40 Managing controlled assessment

"Don't panic!"

Don't get stressed out about controlled assessment. Manage it carefully, avoid breaking the rules and you should be fine.

Plan the use of your time well in advance:

⦿ Decide on the dates of your controlled assessment lessons and share them with your students.

⦿ Do the students need computers for composing? How will you manage the students who will want to move between their instruments and computers? If you have a small number of computers in your classroom, then you can plan some kind of rota for the students who need them. If you don't, then you need to establish how much time you will be able to have in a computer room and then make it clear to the students when they will have access so that they can plan their time.

⦿ Don't forget that controlled assessment time is *write-up* time. Students should be actively encouraged to do much of their thinking and creating beforehand at home. Most exam boards allow for notes/sketches to be brought in provided you can verify that it is the student's work.

⦿ Stress the importance of working on compositions between controlled assessment times so that students can make the most of the time available.

⦿ If you have a large class, can you ask the school for some extra staffing? Can you double the members of staff for the GCSE groups, even for just one or two lessons a week? Every little bit helps.

Top tip

Check the level of control in your specification and don't panic. Don't forget, you simply need to declare authenticity of the students' work, and that it has been completed in the time you have allocated.

Taking it further...

Give the students a log to fill in each time they complete a controlled assessment lesson. It could have an area for notes (some exam boards ask for a detailed log of the composition process) or it could just be a time sheet. If you want to, you can sign it too.

Producing scores 41
for compositions

"I'm going to spend this lesson writing out my composition..."

Spending a lesson writing out a composition is great, and controlled assessment time is mainly about writing up ideas. However, remember some students will need more guidance than others when it comes to producing scores.

Watch out for students who:

● sit at a computer with no notes and expect something to magically appear on the screen

● have written their composition out in letters and are trying to transfer to notation software

● have written a popular composition including drums and guitar and are trying to notate it using notation software.

These students will need support in producing a score that is more appropriate for them. Don't allow your students to think that they will not do as well if they do not notate their composition on staves using traditional Western classical music notation. If this is the student's way of reading and performing, then of course this is the best method for them. However, if your student lacks confidence and ability in this area, don't force them through it or do it for them. Consider other options, e.g.

● Song lyrics written out with note names above, and chord symbols above as well. This can be accompanied by a description of the kind of accompaniment that the guitar/piano will play.

● A detailed written commentary, including dynamics, tempo indications and articulations, where relevant.

You get the idea. A composition score is to give the examiner the best possible way of understanding the student's intentions. Encourage students to be as detailed as they can in all aspects, and to make sure that tempo, dynamics and other details are clear to the examiner.

Bonus idea

Many students struggle with notating the rhythms of their compositions. Try and listen to their composition before they start notating it. You might spot an anacrusis where the student hadn't, and you will be able to double-check their key signature matches the key of their composition, etc.

42 Revision ideas

"How can I make revising fun and engaging?"

In May/June, teachers of music at KS4 and KS5 are faced with an unappetising prospect; it's time to revise until students go on study leave. But do revision lessons have to be so unappealing?

Firstly, don't forget how musical your lessons were when you were introducing the content. If learning is more powerful when students are active and being musical, the same applies when you are revisiting topics and concepts.

Secondly, make it fun!

● Instead of doing practice listening questions as a whole class, try doing them in smaller groups, and turning it into a competition (see Idea 44.)

● Break up several questions into a 'running quiz': give groups or pairs one question at a time, and don't give them the next one until they have answered the first to your satisfaction. Make them run around the room to get the questions, and cause a little chaos.

● Make links – ask students if they can link every set work, or area of study, to every other one, by one common musical feature. See who can get round all the areas or works using the fewest, or most complex, musical features.

● Give students ownership of their revision, and ask them to find related pieces that share musical characteristics with their set music, or get them to find potential tunes for unheard listening (they could even write the questions). Their ear will be challenged by this task, and you will deepen their musical understanding of the style/genre, and its related musical features.

GCSE and A-level surgery 43

"It's called 'revision', not 'vision'."

Offering support outside of lesson time, 'surgery' style, can be the perfect time for some students to consolidate their learning and for you to get to the bottom of any misunderstandings.

GCSE and A-level surgery sessions are great. But what happens if you have a number of students drop in with different needs all in one session? Consider some of the following approaches:

- Be clear that surgery is *not* a replacement for lessons. You don't want students switching off in lessons because they think they will cover it in surgery later on in the week or term.
- Students must take responsibility for their own learning. Insist that they must tell you in advance what they want to cover. Turn them away if they turn up being vague (unless they are very weak students). If they don't have the notes from the lesson, again, turn them away.
- Decide which areas of study/topics you will cover and advertise it to the students. This is particularly useful after a mock exam when you and the students will be able to identify the weakest areas of study.
- Use the quality of classwork, homework and exam results to 'invite' particular students to specific sessions. Inform their parents in parent consultations or give them a call. This kind of intervention will be valuable and also demonstrates you are doing everything to support the student.
- If you know you are going to have a busy session, ask for support from another member of staff in the department, or failing that, split the time into two sessions.

Bonus idea !

Use music captains (see Idea 78) or any older students who have completed their GCSEs or AS levels to support at surgery. If you can, let them know the topic in advance – they will have already covered it themselves but may need some refreshing. Sometimes students just need to hear explanations from their peers in order for it to sink in.

44 Soup up your listening

"Don't ask me how many beats in a bar there are yet again!"

Listening skills are important. Really important. Think about how you can best help your students to improve them.

It is important to remember that students are constantly developing their listening skills as they engage in practical music-making, and that your feedback and guidance will amplify this process. However, sometimes you just need to play them some music, and get them to answer some questions.

Resource books are full of listening worksheets, but the same problems always arise; in a mixed-ability class, some questions will be far too easy, and others totally inaccessible for progressing musicians.

Imagine a listening activity that looks like this:

⦿ Divide the class into groups based on students' current stage of musical development.

⦿ Give each group an iPod (or similar) with a headphone-splitter and several sets of headphones, and a set of questions/tasks tailored to their ability, e.g. ask some students to identify instruments, some to describe simple musical elements, and some to pick out more complex musical features in the music.

⦿ Make the listening a collaborative experience; students discuss within their groups and ask each other questions, making musical decisions and responses in their own time. It is differentiated to maximise the musical progress of every student. They can replay specific sections of the music to ensure they are happy with their responses.

No more silent, drab 'listening starters', with all students staring at the same set of questions, either bored by the second listen, or overwhelmed by the demands made of them.

Taking it further...

The best listening activities improve students' understanding of a piece, genre or style, and then elicit a musical response from them. As well as differentiated questions, give students the opportunity to respond musically to your listening material, again based on their ability, e.g. some students could respond to the overriding emotion of the piece, some could compose using similar musical devices, and others could compose manipulating the conventions of the particular musical style.

BYOD (Bring Your Own Device)

"How can BYOD enhance learning in music?"

There are several ways to include BYOD in your music lessons that will enhance your students' learning in music.

Make music available

Use your blog or Twitter to post resources (e.g. mp3s or PDFs) for your students to access on their phones. Embed them in the post or provide links to Dropbox or Google Drive. This is a huge help if they are in groups learning a piece of music, or composing in a particular style.

Apps

This is a tricky one, because many apps aren't available on both iOS and Android, and many cost money. In a BYOD world, apps are best used as add-ons to practical music-making, rather than as the basis of lessons (use software on computers for this). Here are some possible ideas:

- A free tuner app

- A free piano app

- A free drum machine (or metronome) app

- Chord libraries

- **Apps (such as *TonePad*) that turn your device into an instrument:** again played through amps to enhance group performances, and ensure all students can access practical music-making.

Sheet music

Many well-known providers of sheet music, such as *Sheet Music Direct*, *Musicnotes*, *Songsterr*, and *Ultimate Guitar Tabs*, produce apps allowing you to view sheet music and tabs on mobile devices. A small catalogue of free music is available, but most will need to be purchased.

Top tip

Reinforce the usage policies and expectations of your school's BYOD policy. In the music classroom, with students making noise all over the place, it is difficult to tread the fine line between a positive learning environment, and one in which students abuse the freedoms they are given.

Taking it further...

As well as music-specific apps, don't forget the basic functions of smartphones and tablets. The ability to record is hugely helpful, as is the ability to photograph work and take notes.

46 Storing recordings and automating your department

"Use technology — it will make your life easier!"

Having a huge bank of students' recordings and other work is undoubtedly a good idea. Having recordings stored haphazardly across several devices, with names like '0000123944 12-09-13. mp3', isn't. Think about how you can organise your recordings clearly but quickly.

I used to think that I would sit down at the end of every day, name all the recordings I had made, and sort them into folders. I was unrealistic to say the least! However, technology can make this process a little easier.

Note-taking apps

Many note-taking apps (e.g. *Evernote, Notability, Apple Notes, OneNote*) allow you to make notes that can store any file (e.g. mp3s and images). You can create a note for each class, and record directly into the note. You can then add text around the recordings, or drag in your assessment spreadsheet. In many cases, it can be accessed from anywhere (laptops, phones, web browsers), and is available for free (some features require a paid upgrade). Everything is usually taggable and searchable, and you can share notes easily with your colleagues and your students.

IFTTT (If This, Then That)

IFTTT is a simple concept; if 'this' happens in one app or online service, then do 'that' in another. It uses 'recipes' that can be fully-customised by you.

For example:

○ IF you get an email from a particular person, put it in a particular note in your note-taking app.

○ IF you get a 'high-priority' email, create a task in any number of popular 'to do' apps.

There are countless 'recipes' ready to use, and it is easy to create your own. Check it out.

IFTTT on your smartphone

IFTTT also make a smartphone app that follows a similar principle. You could use it to:

○ Create a 'note' applet that tweets from your Twitter account. Input some text, and it will immediately tweet it, without having to open your Twitter app. The same principle can be used for blog posts, quick reminders, or to append text to a note or document.

○ Create a 'photo' applet and name it after a particular class. Take a photo of some work, and it can automatically add it to a note, a spreadsheet, or anywhere else you want to store it. (Go to **ifttt.com** for more information.)

G Suite for Education

You might need to talk to SLT about this one. It is free for schools and it gives you access to all of Google's cool stuff: sheets, slides, docs, email, drive. It also includes Google Classroom, a kind of fuss-free VLE that allows uploading of work by staff and students, the ability to set assignments, and a safe online forum for discussion and questions. Check out Google Forms for super-easy quizzes, surveys or admin forms. It can really streamline your workflow.

Taking it further...

Create more complex workflows with apps like 'Workflow' for iOS or 'Tasker' for Android. For example, in no time at all I created a simple recording app that knows what class you are teaching. So, you name the recording and it automatically adds it to the Dropbox folder for that specific class. (See my blog post: **playfewernotes. wordpress.com**)

Bonus idea

Scan work. Paper isn't environmentally friendly, and is easily lost. Scan every piece of paper you receive, tag it and name it. Apps like Scannble, Scanbot or ScannerPro are perfect for this. They scan work, make it look beautiful, and store it wherever you want.

47 Department devices

"A small stash of devices."

If, like the majority of us, you are plagued with problems booking out tablets, issues using paid apps on multiple iPads, and patchy Wi-FiTM, then here is a useful approach.

Many departments dismiss new technologies as expensive, fiddly or impractical. However, securing the funds for five or six iPod touches/iPads/cheap tablets can help a department run more smoothly and improve the quality of students' music-making. Find a re-seller offering a good education price, and don't worry about getting the latest generation.

○ Make playlists for A-level, GCSE, and each unit you cover at KS3. Soup up your listening (see Idea 44) and enjoy more engaging and valuable listening activities.

○ Install apps like *TonePad*, *Figure* by Propellerhead, or *DM-1 – The Drum Machine*. During group work, give each group a device connected to an amplifier (some amps, like the *Fender Frontman 10G*, have a dedicated aux in, removing the need for fiddly adaptors). Using the devices as an instrument in performance or composition is a great way of engaging students.

○ Ask students to use devices to make their own recordings, using *Voice Memos* or similar. You then download them to your computer at the end of the day. Make sure students name their recordings carefully, and delete the false starts.

○ Create exemplar materials for your students to listen to whilst in groups.

○ Download the app *FourTrack*. It allows students to loop ideas and record over the top of them – perfect for a student who can't easily notate their complex compositions.

Taking it further...

Make the background of each device a number – this will help you organise and keep track of them. Turn off the camera, and anything else you don't want students to use. Create a separate Apple ID/Google ID from your personal one. Buy a charging dock – they are relatively inexpensive – making the devices easy to store, and ensuring they will always be fully charged and ready to go.

Bonus idea

Apple Configurator is a desktop app used to manage multiple devices on iOS. Talk to your ICT team about licensing multiple app purchases, when you move beyond just using free apps.

Web-based apps 48

"Web-based apps are an easy way into music technology."

If you don't have access to a purpose-built ICT suite, don't give up on using music technology with your students. Web-based apps run in a browser, and only require a connection to the internet. This idea suggests a few to try.

Incredibox (incredibox.com)

This simple game is free. It is a great introduction to sequencing. Students can drag and drop loops, creating simple pieces which they can record.

Soundation (soundation.com) and Soundtrap (soundtrap.com)

These apps are Digital Audio Workstations – DAWs (see Idea 50) in a browser. Free and paid options are available. Students can play with loops and sequence their own original ideas.

Audiotool (audiotool.com)

Audiotool is a more complex program. Again, free and paid options are available. It is a very visual representation of studio effects, synthesisers and drum machines. Reminiscent of the professional software *Reason*, you actually need to wire up your various devices, offering valuable lessons to music technology students

Noteflight (noteflight.com) and Flat.io (flat.io)

This is notation software that exists in a browser. Students can log into *Noteflight* or *Flat* from anywhere, and work on their pieces. Free and paid versions are available. As teacher, you have the ability to see students' work and comment on it in real-time. These apps don't offer all the features of pro-software like *Sibelius* (see Idea 49), but more than enough for most classroom applications.

Top tip

Tutorials, sample lessons, documentaries and how-to guides can all be found on video-hosting sites like YouTube.

Taking it further...

Soundation and *Noteflight* are available through *MusicFirst* (see Idea 10), which offers storage for recordings, the ability to assign assessments to students, collaboration and much more. *Soundtrap* and *Flat* work well with *Google's Education Suite* (see Idea 49), which allows live collaboration and commenting on students' work. *Soundtrap* also has a useful iOS app.

49 Notation software

"Notation software is like a word processor for music."

For students who are familiar with Western notation, or are learning to be familiar with it, notation software is an essential. It is worth taking the time to choose software that best suits your students.

Many schools sit their students down with notation software and ask them to compose. The danger of this is that you end up with 'clicking composers', whose pieces lack musicality. Always encourage your students to start their composing and creativitity with instruments. The notation software is more like a word-processor for music, to record rather than create the ideas.

Sibelius

Sibelius is the behemoth of notation software and the favoured choice of professionals, so it seems the go-to choice. It is great piece of kit. But this doesn't mean it is the best choice for students. It can be far too complex, buggy on networks, and prohibitively expensive. Recently subscription and outright purchase options have become available, which may help schools with tight budgets. However, there are other software options to consider.

Finale

This is another industry standard. Choosing between *Sibelius* and *Finale* is a bit like the age-old Mac versus PC debate. It depends what you were brought up with, and what you know.

Notion

Made by PreSonus, *Notion* is a new kid on the block. It prides itself on its sounds (recorded by the LSO and other professional studio musicians) and its affordability. It is cheap (though can be pricey when you add up additional sounds costs), and also available on mobile devices, allowing you to edit on-the-go. They make a piece of specific tab software, *Progression*, which is a great add-on for guitarists.

Noteflight and Flat.io (web-based)

Web-based notation software (see Idea 48, <XREF>) has many advantages. A school licence is often available for a fraction of the price of software that needs to be installed. Students can work anywhere with a browser, so you can book computer rooms that don't have *Sibelius* up and running. Collaboration is key; students can send you work, you can comment and change in real time. They often lack the features and sounds of more expensive software, but they are worth checking out for most school uses.

MuseScore

MuseScore is free, and open-source. It is updated regularly (which can be annoying on a school network), and works with a drag and drop system that some students really take to. It can't compete on features or sounds, and by its nature is full of bugs. However, it is easy to use, and also costs nothing.

Taking it further...

The list of software options is endless. Check out *NoteWorthy Composer*, *Forte*, *MagicScore*, *QuickScore*, or *StaffPad*. Read online reviews and talk to colleagues and sales reps.

Bonus idea

Networks. This tip applies to most ideas in the technology section. Music software rarely works well with networked computers in schools. If you have the opportunity, standalone computers run music software more reliably. The perceived disadvantage is that students always need to log on to the same computer. However, this can be addressed using Google Drive, Dropbox and other online storage options.

50 DAWs (Digital Audio Workstations)

"Digital Audio Workstations can broaden the opportunities for music-making in your school."

Technology is an integral part of music education. We have moved beyond just using *Sibelius* as a musical word-processing tool, and now use technology to enhance the musical learning of our students. DAWs, sequencers, whatever you want to call them, can allow all students to create music, avoiding barriers like notation, or instrumental ability. However, they can be expensive, temperamental or confusing.

Here is a brief outline of DAWs for schools:

GarageBand and Logic

This is a popular choice if you have Macs, otherwise it is a no-go. Lots of schools use *GarageBand* at KS3, before moving on to *Logic* at KS4 and KS5. This is sensible; both have high-quality loops, allow you to use effects, and sequence music with ease. They are incredibly user-friendly. However, the set-up is expensive, as is the *Logic* software. While *GarageBand* is fairly fool-proof, *Logic* can take time to learn, but it is totally worth it when you crack it.

Cubase

If you have a Windows set-up, *Cubase* is a popular choice. It is of professional quality, which has its pros and cons in terms of usability. Steinberg, who make *Cubase*, make several additional pieces of software, including add-ons, smartphone apps and stripped-down versions of the full suite. This can be helpful if you have a limited budget, or confusing if you are looking to inherit a system with several versions of *Cubase* installed. *Cubase* is a popular choice if you are lucky enough to have a recording studio in your department.

StudioOne

Made by PreSonus, the *StudioOne* suite is a new arrival on the DAW scene. Similar to *Cubase* and *Logic*, it is very competitively priced, and can be geared specifically towards schools. They also make the notation software *Notion*, which links well with *StudioOne.* They have staff employed specifically to work with schools.

Soundation/AudioTool/Soundtrap

These three web apps that can be used for free, are detailed in Idea 48. They are less powerful than software installed on your machines, but easier to access. They are great for 'hooking' students in, before moving on to more complex programs.

Ableton Live and Reason

Focussed more on live performance, and DJ'ing, these pieces of software encourage creative use of effects and sampling. The interface isn't for everyone, but can feel more hands-on, due to the unique visual approaches. These pieces of software are probably used more to enhance a set-up, rather than to act as your core program.

Taking it further...

Don't make the mistake of just using DAWs to click in MIDI tunes, and draw lines on a screen. Ensure your set-up allows students to perform with music technology; whether this is with a MIDI keyboard, a simple audio interface, or a full-blown recording studio. Make sure your use of technology is *musical*, with students making *musical* decisions and being creative, rather than just going through the motions of using a piece of software.

Bonus idea

There are more solutions than those listed here. The next time you get a catalogue in your pigeonhole, talk to their sales rep. Many companies will provide trial copies, or a few licences to test, before you break the bank on the ideal solution.

51 Music and computing

"Coding sound is a black box for me."

Taking it further...

Up-skilling to master the basics of *Sonic Pi*, though surprisingly straightforward, can take time that you may not have. Enlist the help of your ICT or technology departments and IT support staff; they can help you write and deliver a scheme of work, and everybody wins.

Bonus idea

Music notation, in any form, is a language just like code. Once you have learnt the basic rules, and how to understand the particular symbols and syntax, you are ready to experiment and be creative. If you are making your own resources for music and computing projects, examples that students can listen to, then edit, are key. A blank screen could put off even the keenest budding programmer/ composer.

Music and computing is not about using music technology (think sound recording, or software like Cubase or GarageBand). It is about using music as the 'subject matter' for a project or scheme of work on code. Music can provide an exciting and accessible way in to coding.

Sonic Pi is a free, open-source project developed by Sam Aaron and Cambridge University. It can easily be installed onto any machine, and allows students to making sound using just one line of code. *Sonic Pi* allows you to do the following:

- Create dance music using computer-generated drum beats and synthesisers.

- Combine the software with physical buttons and dials to create 'instruments' that students can play.

- Code traditional melody, harmony and rhythm, as well as more abstract soundscapes.

- Create music that embraces randomness, and sounds different every time it is played.

- Perform music live by writing code in real time.

Sonic Pi is a growing project; lots of resources and schemes of work already exist for it, and more are being written all the time. 'Coding schools' are popping up all over the country – these are holiday courses that teach students to code at a high level in a matter of days. Consider *Sonic Pi* as an exciting new direction in your curriculum.

Repertoire choices 52

"It's all about picking the right pieces."

Selecting music that sounds good but also challenges students can be difficult. Students often like to perform music they know, but your job should also be to introduce them to music they don't know and that they will eventually come to love.

Get the balance right

Select some music in a style that they are familiar with (or even music they know) alongside new and challenging repertoire. They will be able to learn some music quickly, giving them a sense of achievement, but also feel musically challenged by your choices too.

Tailor choices to your ensemble

Each year your ensembles will be different. Make sure that what you choose is performable by your students. Sometimes, plucking arrangements off the shelf (well, downloading them from the internet) without looking through them carefully can catch you out. If you have strengths in specific sections, then find music that caters for this, for example if you have a strong tenor section (if so, how did you get them?!), then consider the *Agnus dei* from Fauré's *Requiem* which showcases them beautifully. On the other hand, if you don't have an oboe player, don't programme the famous *Scene* from Tchaikovsky's *Swan Lake*.

Be realistic

You will probably be working towards an end-of-term concert. If you think some of your pieces won't be ready, then make sure you have pieces that can be prepared in this time. By all means don't give up after one attempt at a piece, but don't be afraid to leave a piece if it isn't going anywhere.

Taking it further...

If you can't find the right piece or arrangement, consider writing your own. You will be able to tailor it to your ensemble, assigning more difficult parts to challenge your more able, whilst giving simpler parts to others.

Bonus idea

Choose music about which you are passionate – it will inspire the students. Give them some context surrounding the music they perform and many of them will go off and listen to more of the same.

53 Rehearsal techniques

"I always play through something at the beginning and something at the end."

It doesn't matter how good an ensemble is or how much detail you want to go into, framing a rehearsal of a piece with a run through at the beginning and the end gives the students an idea of how the music fits together. It will also (hopefully) demonstrate the improvement made during the rehearsal.

Playing through to start

Even if the students are sight-reading, keep counting or leading from the piano (and singing through everything you can and shouting out rehearsal markings!) and let them stumble through it. Congratulate them at the end for getting through it. You will now know where to start!

Say something positive

No one wants to hear just a constant stream of criticism or list of points for improvement, so make sure that you praise at least one element before offering your pearls of wisdom.

Pencils

Make sure your students bring pencils to mark up bowing, breath marks and anything else. If they make the same mistake again (they definitely will!), you can at least point out that it's in their music! If you are teaching music by rote, then your physical gestures will be key to them changing their musical response.

Demonstrate what you want

If it's a choir rehearsal, sing to your students; if it's an instrumental rehearsal, then use an instrument to demonstrate what you want. Failing that, sing! Students often learn best by copying and this is no different in a rehearsal situation. You can always use your older or more advanced students to demonstrate too.

Go over the changes/improvements you have made

Once you have made changes, then go over the passage again. It sounds obvious but many people don't do this. Students need time to absorb changes and adapt. You might have to do it more than once again. Make it clear why you are doing something again: 'This is for the crescendo I want in bar 9'.

Sometimes you just need to do it again

Don't feel that after every run through you have to say something to make it better. Going over the same passage a few times is sometimes exactly what the students need, especially at the start of the process.

Always finish your rehearsal with a run through of a piece or a section of a piece. If you have pieces you want to keep ticking over, this is a good time to go through them.

Taking it further...

Plan sectional rehearsals where you ask other members of staff or senior students to lead small rehearsals with individual parts. Progress will be quicker and it gives students a bit more time to absorb the music they are learning.

Bonus idea

Get an 'expert' in to take the odd rehearsal. It could be an instrumental teacher or, if you can afford it, a local professional. Sometimes the students just need to hear the same thing but from someone different.

54 Conducting instrumental ensembles

"It's not just about keeping time."

Keeping time is in fact the easiest part. You can easily learn how to move your arms mechanically in the right direction, but that's only the beginning. Students respond better to a musical conductor than they do to musical instructions on their music.

Conducting is about communicating your musical intentions. Here are some tips on how to get beyond the basics:

Eye contact

This applies to any type of conducting or leading, instrumental or choral. An encouraging look is the most effective way to bring a student in.

Top tip

You have to put yourself out there. Be passionate about the music which you are conducting and demonstrate it through your gestures, e.g. move your arms legato for students to play legato. You will be surprised by how your students subconsciously respond.

Taking it further...

For more ideas, read books, go on courses and, of course, observe professional conductors when you attend concerts.

Big down beat

Whatever you are performing, students will need a big down beat (and often a big up beat). Make your down beat clear, big and definite in forte passages, and in quieter passages, give a smaller beat, but make sure your down beat bounces up from an imaginary point.

Know your score well

If your head is stuck in your score, you won't be looking up at your players, so you can't expect them to look at you. Use both arms so you can keep time and bring players in. Don't get obsessed by keeping time. If you 'let go' for a few beats here and there, the music is unlikely to fall apart or stop. Instil an internal pulse in your players (see Idea 8).

Conducting big bands/popular ensembles

Having a drummer who keeps time, means you won't need to show the beat all the time (though that does depend on the drummer, of course!). With styles such as jazz, you will often be helping players play off-beat stabs in time, or syncopated phrases together and bringing out nuances in the music.

Conducting choirs

"Conducting choirs; a different beast!"

Singing is very personal. The students don't have instruments behind which they can hide, and the less experienced will often sing without support, while the more confident may dominate the texture. Getting the balance right is key, but takes a lot of time.

As well as taking on board the points from Idea 54, consider the following:

Internal pulse

The internal pulse of a choir can be one of the most frustrating things you deal with (even with an accompanist). Whilst waving your hands in time will not necessarily improve this, constant shouting of the beat during their singing will definitely bring it to their attention! Make your peace with the fact that singers simply don't come in dead on the beat like instrumentalists do and accommodate that into your direction.

Gestures

There's more to life than just bringing the students off at the end of the phrase. How will you get your singers to achieve the phrase shapes you want? If the choir is going flat, how will you conduct in order to change their sound? Have an experiment and you will often find that smaller gestures lower down will encourage your students to support their sound, and that creating the shape of an arch as they sing will get them to consider the shapes of their phrases.

Accompanist

Are you a good enough pianist to score-read and lead a rehearsal from the piano? The flow of the rehearsal will certainly be at its best if you are in control of everything. However, it will also depend on the experience of a choir. If they need leading, then find a more experienced accompanist.

Taking it further...

As in the previous idea, these ideas merely scratch the surface of choral conducting. You don't have to be an expert to get the best out of your choirs, but there are lots of experienced conductors out there from whom you can learn. Check out A&C Black's *Inspire Your Choir* as your first port of call.

56 Productions

"I always make friends with the drama department!"

If you've never put on a school musical before, then start thinking. The journey that you go on with the cast, band and crew is incredible, and the results are unbelievably rewarding.

Having a good working relationship with your drama department is key to putting on the best production possible. You need to be on the same page and support each other when times get difficult; communication is key. Make sure you consider:

○ **Time frame:** When is the best time for your departments to put on a production without having a huge impact on pressure points? When will you start rehearsing and how many times a week? Select your rehearsal days and times carefully: consider the commitments of your 'target students'.

○ **Type of show:** Who's going to be in it? Is it going to be all-inclusive with a huge cast? Or will it be a smaller, more select cast, who you want to push and challenge? Consider the students you have in both departments and their strengths. The male-female ratio will need to be considered in terms of choice of show: *Guys and Dolls*, *Oliver* and *Joseph*, for example, require a lot of boys. Do you have them?

○ **Performing rights:** Search for who owns the rights to your chosen show and make an application as early as you can. Decide what kind of band you will have (you will be offered a variety of parts) and how early in advance you will need your scripts and band parts (typically released only a month or two before).

○ **Get the whole school involved:** From set design through to front-of-house, staff and students from other departments can get involved, giving a wider sense of ownership of the production.

Top tip

Create a detailed rehearsal schedule from the outset and stick to it. If things don't get covered or rehearsals don't happen, reschedule immediately. And be positive. Of course hold students to account if they haven't learnt songs or lines, but then give them something back when it goes well. Show the students your best side, and they will show you theirs.

48-hour musical

"Mad? Yes. Fun? Totally."

Many music and drama departments are not able put on a joint production every year, and often do it biannually. Here's a solution for what to do in the interim year: stage a 48-hour musical. Start on Friday at 1 p.m. and perform on Sunday at 6 p.m.!

Persuade your site team to open up parts of the school for you to rehearse over the weekend. Ask for permission to start on a Friday afternoon from lunchtime, and get the students off timetable. The hours could be Friday 1 p.m.–9 p.m., Saturday 10 a.m.–8 p.m. and Sunday 10 a.m.–6 p.m. (performance at 6 p.m.).

Beforehand

Choose a show for which the music is relatively simple, so students can listen to it beforehand. Hold the usual auditions in advance of the show and cast it as you would any other show. Hand out scripts and scores in advance and make it clear that all songs and lines must be learnt in advance of the weekend. Create a schedule for the weekend: if you can open up different departments, you can have dance, acting and music rehearsals all happening at the same time!

During the weekend

As with a 'normal' musical, stick to the rehearsal schedule and make sure you have 'mopping up' sessions for when things don't go to plan. Make sure there are as many rehearsals going on as possible, but that time is left for it all to get put together. Just because it's a 48-hour musical, don't assume that standards can't be high. Forget the time frame and set your expectations high, and your students will deliver.

> **Top tip**
>
> There may be times throughout the weekend when students are waiting around. Make sure you have prepped them for this; homework can be done, as well as much relaxing and socialising with students in other years. Also, appoint a group of responsible upper-school students (for example, your music captains, see Idea 78) who you can trust to take smaller rehearsals or work with individual students. Call on them to take on students who you feel need extra help.

58 Music tour

"The music tour was an unforgettable musical experience!"

Think back to music tours, band residentials or choir trips you went on as a young musician. Music tours offer unique performing opportunities, as well as the chance for students to make new friends and visit exciting new places. Start planning your first music tour today!

As well as being exciting, music tours do of course also create a lot of work and additional stress – but they are usually worth it!

Here are a few things to consider when planning a music tour:

○ **Tour companies:** At an additional cost, tour companies can take a lot of the hard work off you. They can secure your venues, travel and accommodation, provide you with a city guide and book your excursions.

○ **Who to take:** Are you going to open your tour to everyone, and then allocate ensembles? A combination of vocal and instrumental ensembles works well.

○ **Where to go:** If you only have singers, you can fly (if your students can afford it). If you have instruments, you need a coach, and probably a trailer. Whilst journeys of over twenty hours across Europe may seem daunting, they provide your students with a unique bonding experience. They will probably talk about the journey more than the concerts!

Taking it further...

Start small, and grow. Your first tour will have fewer musicians, and you might need to pick a more straightforward repertoire. As long as the music is good, the tour will be great. Consider a tour which includes workshops with different professionals to provide students with a fresh insight into music-making.

○ Where to perform: Churches have great acoustics which provide a memorable performing opportunity, but they can restrict repertoire, and are cold if you go in the winter. Retirement homes allow all ensembles to perform, but audiences can be quietly appreciative. Open-air concerts always draw a crowd, but only if the weather is right. You could consider performing at regular masses, or at special events like the nightly remembrance service at the Menin Gate in Ypres, Belgium.

○ When to go: It will cost students less if you don't go during the holidays. The last week of term might work if your school allows it. February half term doesn't impact too much on exams, but it is cold if you stay in Europe. Easter could work, as you can give yourself a week to recover, although some students might prefer to stay home ahead of examination season.

○ What to do: Tour companies will have a list of excursions, such as food-tasting sessions, water parks, factory tours, boat rides, etc. There are also museusm and exhibitions. Plan a varied programme, but make sure the emphasis is on the music. A rehearsal slot in the first day or two will help settle nerves, and a quiz or games night in your hostel or hotel helps bring people together at no cost.

Top tip

Think carefully about timings. You don't want to be rushing to a venue five minutes before you are likely to perform. It is better to arrive in plenty of time, so leave breathing room in your schedule. Visiting venues before the tour can really help; you will know where the coach can park, who to talk to and exactly where you will be performing. Students enjoy some free time in cities, but not too much, so plan accordingly.

59 Arts Award

"The Arts Award is fantastic for bringing the arts together."

This is a great way of getting more than just your 'usual suspects' involved in the arts. The only criterion should be a passion for one or more of the arts and the desire to explore this passion.

Since its launch in 2005, Trinity College have given out more than 200,000 awards to young people across the UK. The Arts Award gives young people of all abilities a chance to engage with and deepen their understanding within the arts, as well as develop creative thinking and leadership skills. Depending on the level, students create projects and events, driven by their passion and moderated and advised by a member of staff at the school (who needs to have been trained as an Arts Award advisor).

Benefits

The Arts Award is a national qualification, with UCAS points also awarded to those who achieve Gold level. Students have a lot of fun in the process and their understanding of the arts is most certainly deepened during the process. As a school, having students take part in the programme raises the profile of your department and also gives you an opportunity to engage students who would not otherwise have a huge passion for your subject.

Levels

As well as the Bronze, Silver, and Gold Awards (Levels 1, 2 and 3 respectively on the Qualifications and Credit Framework), young people can also take part in the two introductory levels, Discover and Explore.

Advisors and costs

In order to run the Arts Award at your school, you must have a qualified advisor who will moderate the students' work. Training courses are run throughout the year. The cost of these varies from year to year. Your moderations will also be checked by someone at Trinity, who will visit your centre (postal moderation is available where there only a few participants).

There is a cost for entering the students (see **artsaward.org.uk**). You need to decide whether you will bear this cost, or whether you will ask the students to cover it.

Who takes part and when?

Some schools offer it to students on an extra-curricular basis, asking each of the arts departments to select appropriate students from a specific year group to take part in one of the levels. Sessions are then held outside curriculum time and it becomes a good project for independent learning as much as anything else.

Other schools run it as part of the curriculum, often in Year 9, when enthusiasm and motivation can become varied in the lead-up to GCSE options. In this case, there is often more of a corporate approach, for example everyone will go and see the same arts event and review it in the same way, or everyone in the year group will take part in the same arts activity in lesson time.

Top tip

Roll out the Arts Award year by year. For example, start with a small cohort of Year 8 students and run the Bronze Award in the first year, with a view to doing the same the next year, but adding Silver Award in Year 9.

Taking it further...

Contact other local secondary schools and see if they are running the Arts Award. Sharing ideas and approaches will be valuable, and you can also apply for joint moderations if you are low in numbers.

60 Flagship ensembles

"There's nothing like the frisson of excitement after a set of auditions for the chamber choir or big band!"

Top tip

Don't forget the key rule: the members of your selective ensembles should ideally remain members of their larger counterpart. It's a new challenge for them, but it doesn't make them 'better' than the others. They still need to do their bit.

Taking it further...

Prepare your students for your flagship ensembles by creating a 'training' ensemble, an auditioned ensemble in between your non-auditioned group and your chamber group. This works very well for choirs. In a training ensemble, you can focus on sound, singing in more parts and more accuracy, which can be harder to achieve in your non-auditioning main choir.

Creating an ensemble for which membership is selected through auditions, will raise the aspirations of the students in the department and, more importantly, give your more experienced musicians a real challenge.

Repertoire

When you've got more confident readers and performers, challenge them with your repertoire choices. If you want to open their ears to new styles, mix them in with styles that are more familiar. Variety is key here. You don't want to scare them off with a lot of challenging repertoire, but part of your job is surely to broaden their musical horizons and they will love it.

How many? How old? How 'good'?

If your flagship ensemble is instrumental, then that generally answers the first question. Whilst your older students are more likely to be more experienced, your flagship ensemble is also the perfect place to stretch your gifted students at any age.

When auditioning, you should also consider students who show potential but might not be ready yet. Be flexible; if you have a large cohort leaving next year, plan for progression. Accepting students who show potential but aren't quite ready will let them learn from the most experienced students and grow into their roles when the older students leave.

"My students love big bands and all that jazz."

Most schools have a big band, or something resembling a big band. They are fantastic ensembles, especially if run properly.

Here are some top tips for getting the most out of your big band.

Improvisation

Encourage improvisation. Invite the rhythm section and soloists for a rehearsal, and get them to build up their confidence improvising in small groups. Then let them strut their stuff in front of the whole band.

Warm-up

Play a simple tune like Duke Ellington's *C Jam Blues* at the start of a rehearsal, and get everyone to improvise over the twelve-bar blues. It's a great warm-up!

Instrumentation

In a secondary school music department, all of the following are acceptable: bass lines written as tab for a guitarist; clarinets on the trumpet or tenor sax parts; French horns or bassoons on trombone parts; keyboard players playing pretty much any part.

Encourage clarinettists to rent or buy tenor saxes, or lend them if you have them. Aim to develop a culture of big band musicians; it will flourish over time.

Repertoire

Play everything: jazz, funk, blues, Latin, pop, charts. You name it, it sounds good in a big band.

Sub-groups

Have ensembles 'branching out' from the main big band, e.g. a 'little' big band, a saxophone group, a brass group (traditional or 'New Orleans' style with marching percussion), a soul band, or a smaller jazz combo.

Top tip

Publishers Hal Leonard and Alfred Music have an enormous library of big band music, clearly arranged by difficulty, with listening tracks to preview before you buy.

Taking it further...

A jazz 'dinner dance' can be a huge money spinner. A few nice tablecloths, some candles (real or fake depending on health and safety), and canapés organised by the parents' association can quickly turn into a lucrative annual event.

62 School orchestras

"We play everything, from Memory from Cats to Tchaikovsky's Nutcracker."

The numbers in your school 'orchestra' and the balance of instruments will most certainly depend on your school's intake and their interests. But there is no reason why you can't start with some kind of instrumental ensemble and build up from there.

Taking it further...

If you want to keep your school orchestra as a mainly inclusive group, consider setting up chamber instrumental ensembles. You may want to set up a chamber orchestra, or even divide groups up into senior strings, woodwind ensemble and brass ensemble.

Instrumentation

Decide what kind of ensemble you are running. Is it a non-auditioning all-inclusive ensemble for students on any instrument to join, or are you going for as close to the instrumentation of a traditional orchestra as possible? If you have the resources, allowing as many strings as possible into the orchestra and then auditioning or selecting your more advanced woodwind and brass players will stretch the group musically. If you have lots of woodwind and brass players, then make sure you have a concert band or wind band in which they can all play.

Repertoire

Like everything else, this of course depends on your ensemble. Selecting music that is too challenging can deflate instrumentalists, and finding music too easy can put them off. Choosing a good repertoire for a school orchestra is more about selecting the appropriate arrangements. Choose the original of Mussorgsky's *Night on a Bare Mountain* and the students won't make it through in one piece, whereas if you find a good amateur arrangement (taking out a lot of extended woodwind, brass and percussion), not only will they enjoy rehearsing it, you will have introduced them to something new. That said, if your orchestra is up to it, then tackling an original orchestration can be extremely satisfying.

Where to find music

○ *Kaleidoscope*: If your school orchestra is just starting out or varies in instrumentation, then consider the *Kaleidoscope* arrangements with their melody, part 1/part 2/part 3 etc. parts written in C, B flat and E flat. These can be found from all good music distributors.

○ *Good music* (goodmusicpublishing. co.uk): Has excellent arrangements (most are similar to original orchestrations but with simplified string parts) of many well-known works from the orchestral repertoire.

○ *Studio Music* (studio-music.co.uk): Has very good arrangements, especially of modern film themes and pop arrangements too. You can also find arrangements according to ability.

○ *IMSLP: Petrucci Music Library* (imslp.org): Has original orchestral scores by composers who are no longer in copyright.

○ Your local library: Every county should have a music or performing arts library. You can set up an account and borrow parts for a small charge.

○ Borrow: Don't forget about your local schools and amateur orchestras. Borrowing each other's scores and parts will save you a lot of time and money, as well as providing the students with an opportunity to explore a wider repertoire.

Top tip

Make sure the students sign out the parts and you know who is responsible for what. Parts going missing are a real source of stress for teachers, so at least minimise it by being organised.

63 Boys and singing

"How do I deal with loud trebles, groaners, and getting them in the door in the first place?"

Starting a boys' choir isn't difficult. It is important. Here are some valuable lessons learned from running a successful (non-auditioned) male voice choir (or as the cool kids call it, MVC) in a mixed state comprehensive for several years.

When you start your choir, don't make the mistake of thinking you will grow it from Year 7. Boys will lose interest, and they won't have anyone to look up to. Find your best musicians from across the years. Drag them off the playground if you have to. Get them to bring their mates. Some will require a bit of persuasion, but will soon discover the joy of singing in a choir.

A burgeoning male voice choir will be mainly sopranos, basses and misfits (SBM). This isn't a selection to be found on many sheet music websites, so arrangements can be hard to come by. Two-part arrangements work well, and SAB can work if you have enough boys who can hold an alto line. Don't worry too much about which octave boys are singing in.

Finding pieces with a solo line and adding simple harmonies is another excellent way of finding repertoire for your boys. It is more important to get the boys singing confidently and expressively, than to worry about blend and ensemble sound (at least at first).

The male voice choir is always a hit at end of term concerts. The sight of boys singing (and hopefully enjoying it) is a guaranteed crowd-pleaser. Don't beat yourself up if they are a little rough around the edges.

Taking it further...

Slow and steady progress is good in any new choir, particularly if you have a group of boys new to singing. If you get a couple of tenors and a couple of basses who can confidently hold a line, get some barbershop arrangements. Then you can really stretch your more able singers, and your concert gets another item that will inspire more boys to start singing.

Extra-curricular stretching

"Allow your students to flourish in a mixed-ability extra-curricular programme."

How can you stretch gifted students in your extra-curricular programme? Not easy, is it?

Just having the best students in one ensemble, with hard music, and the beginners in another, is troubling, for several reasons:

○ A two-tier system with students separated by ability is problematic, and not very inclusive.

○ Students are more inspired by better musicians in weekly rehearsals than in one termly concert (that they might not even see).

○ Playing harder repertoire is not the only way to stretch a gifted musician.

Here are some alternative approaches:

○ Choose pieces that give more able musicians the chance to shine in a larger ensemble. Pieces that feature soloists, sections, or even movements from concerti could work.

○ Have students lead warm-ups. Particularly if they have just been on a band or choir course, they can bring back the warm-ups they learned there, to benefit all students.

○ Have students lead sectionals. They can then pass on their skills to less experienced musicians.

○ Consult with students about repertoire choice and rehearsal planning.

○ Give them the challenge of taking up a related instrument, e.g. alto clarinet, bass clarinet, baritone saxophone, flugelhorn, double bass, vibraphone, etc.

○ Ask them to lead an ensemble (see Idea 65).

○ Encourage them to attend county or national courses, and audition for more prestigious ensembles.

Taking it further...

Have auditioned ensembles alongside your inclusive groups (see Idea 61).

Bonus idea

Be mindful of the culture in your department. There is a fine line between a role model and a diva. Don't let anyone get too big-headed – they probably aren't quite as good as they think they are. Keep them in check!

65 Student-led ensembles

"Give your older students new experiences."

If you can see a gap in your extra-curricular provision but can't find the time to run the ensemble, then consider offering it to an older student to run.

Asking your students to lead a small ensemble broadens their musical experiences outside performing and composing, challenging them in new ways. The student you choose could be one of your music captains (see Idea 78), but it doesn't have to be. Find the most suitable person in terms of instrumental experience and personality (not always the same person!).

Monitoring versus intervention?

This really depends on how the student responds to the challenge. If they have recruited well and have chosen suitable repertoire for their group, then you may well be fine with the odd conversation and popping into rehearsals now and then. If their group is not very well attended, this is often an indication that the student needs your help. You may find that you need to re-recruit, help select some repertoire and be heavily involved in rehearsals for a while. If you are unable to manage it, can someone else in your department help out here?

Performing opportunities

If the group is ready for an end-of-term concert, then go for it and put them in. If they are developing well but need more time, then don't push them. You might find other opportunities for them (you never know when your school association or governing body might want some background performers, etc.) but make sure they are ready for whatever they play in.

Taking it further...

If you or your colleagues are ever unable to take a rehearsal of a bigger ensemble, why not give it to a student to do? If you think it will be logistically difficult, ask a member of staff to drop in and supervise.

"If you like that, you'll like this..."

Pointing students in the direction of relevant wider listening has never been easier. Music is at their fingertips: Spotify, YouTube, Apple Music... But your students still need guidance.

Composer of the week

Have music playing in the entrance hall or foyer in your department (or failing that, your classroom). Put up composer of the week posters with a few facts and dates. Play a selection by this composer between lessons, at break, lunchtime and after school. Even if the response is, 'Who on earth is this?', and students are only listening in the queue for the instrument cupboard, you will get them talking and be able to at least engage in a discussion and share a few more facts and information with them.

'Bookends'

This is popular with GCSE students. Start or end the lesson with a personal favourite of yours and explain why. It doesn't have to be related to music they might be studying – you can just play an excerpt of something which you have enjoyed getting to know. Students appreciate the personal touch and some will go off and listen to more of the same.

Bedtime listening

Set up bedtime listening on Twitter. I have been posting bedtime listening every night between 9 p.m. and 10.30 p.m. on Twitter for nearly five years (#BeaumontBedtimeListening). It is often dedicated to a year group or an ensemble, often related to what they are studying or playing. If nothing 'relevant' comes to mind, then simply pluck a track from your music collection and share!

> **Top tip**
>
> Even if you think no one is listening to or reading your tweets, keep going and remain consistent. Talk about it in lessons (you will be surprised how many students will actually have listened to your track) or set it as homework, with some follow-up questions in the lesson. Make sure you choose a variety of styles to engage all kinds of students. There's nothing wrong with Schubert one night, followed by some Disney the next. Music is music, and students need to be exposed to as much as possible.

67 Curriculum enrichment days

"Today we're going to do something different."

Your school probably has a number of days a year where everyone goes off timetable to do enrichment activities in a variety of subjects. See them as an opportunity to provide more students with musical experiences they otherwise wouldn't have.

This is the perfect opportunity for you to get some professionals in and introduce musical styles that you might not cover in your curriculum. Samba, African drumming or gamelan; there will by plenty of organisations and groups who specialise in running workshops for schools, but will obviously come with a fee. If your school's enrichment budget can foot the bill, fantastic, otherwise asking the students for a small payment may have to be an option.

If you can't find people who will come to you, is there anywhere local you can explore? If you are close to London, the South Bank Centre holds free gamelan workshops but they aren't the only ones. If you live in a university town, the music faculty may run workshops and, of course, your local hub may run something similar.

Alternatively, stay in school and try and give the students something you wouldn't usually offer in the curriculum. If you've got those steel pans lurking, now's the time to dust them off and get them out! If you don't run a 'Battle of the bands', this could be the time to give it a go (in a day!). Or, can you get down to the gym and see if you can get the basketballs out and come up with some rhythm routines à la *High School Musical* (but better!)?

> **Bonus idea**
>
> If there are any notable achievements from the day, celebrate them in assemblies, lessons and in the school community. Videoing or recording performances for future viewing is good fun, or if you have created some kind of competition, can winners gain points for their houses or forms?

Inter-form competitions

"Finish your schemes of work four weeks early in the summer term."

Let's face it, the final slog towards the end of the school year can be pretty grim, especially if you teach Year 9 through to the end of the year. Get rid of that end-of-year feeling and create an inter-form competition within each of your KS3 year groups.

Tell students that, as a class, they need to prepare the following for the inter-form competition:

◉ a class performance of a song of their choice (everyone in the class must be involved in this)

◉ a small ensemble performance

◉ a solo performance

◉ a PowerPoint presentation to be projected and played through the performance (e.g. pictures of the rehearsal process, contributions from the class, etc.).

Whether you include rules about only having live performances, or only having student accompanists, is entirely up to you and will depend on the students you have. If you want to set a theme, then go for it. Give the students a number of lessons to prepare their performances, using the resources you have available. Your role can simply be to facilitate and monitor what should be a good independent learning project, and to motivate and coordinate the students where necessary.

Each form then presents their performances to a panel of selected judges chosen by you (consider members of SLT, members of staff and even alumni). They can score each performance and reveal the overall results at the end of the competition. This is a great way to involve more students in making music which is not part of the curriculum, and you never know who you might pick up for your clubs if you do a nice rousing speech at the end!

Top tip

Make sure you check through song lyrics and themes and ensure they are appropriate for school performances. As well as the other members of your department, call in help from the teachers who would have been teaching the classes on the day. If you have a strong house system, this works brilliantly as a House music competition as well.

69 Staff Grade-1-a-thon

"I really wished I had learnt an instrument when I was younger..."
(random member of staff)

Well here's your chance! The Grade-1-a-thon can be the perfect way to raise the profile of your department, as well as spreading the musical love around the school.

The Grade-1-a-thon is a well-known scheme that encourages people to sign up for instrumental/voice lessons with a view to becoming approximately Grade 1 standard by the end of the process (search Grade-1-a-thon at abrsm.org for a brief overview and resource pack). Give your students the opportunity to teach and members of staff the opportunity to learn! You may prefer to organise this all yourself, but if you have music captains (see Idea 78) or prefects, this is the perfect job for them!

❍ Have a bank of students at the ready to be the teachers. Depending on how advanced they are, get a feel for who wants to be involved and to commit to the project.

❍ Ask members of staff to sign up with a preferred instrument (let them select from a list you have provided). Collect an entry fee – a suggested amount is about £10 for the year. This will cover purchases such as music, reeds, strings, etc. Any proceeds can go to your music department or a charity of the students' choice.

❍ Beg and borrow instruments from the school community and beyond. Try and get hold of as many instruments as you can free of charge. Parents and teachers often have instruments lurking in their attics. Otherwise, ask your local hub, instrumental teachers or other schools for spare instruments.

● See if your local hub will donate you some practice books.

● Give some basic training to your student teachers. Don't assume that just because they can play an instrument, they will be able to pass on their skills easily. Encourage them to plan their lessons in the way we would plan ours and to be patient with their learners. Adult learners are slower than they will anticipate.

● Check in on the process every month or so (or get your captains to) to see if both student teachers and adult learners feel comfortable.

● Give the learners a focus point – organise a date for a big Grade-1-a-thon concert. Closer to the time, decide who will perform solos or who will perform in small ensembles. Organise a Grade-1-a-thon orchestra in which everyone can play; the adult learners can learn the music in their instrumental lessons.

● For everyone who makes it to the end of the process, award them some kind of certificate at the concert.

It feels like a lot of organising at the start, but it will be worth it! You can even take part yourself! The benefits are clear. Not only does this raise the profile of your department, but more importantly it allows for students and teachers to see each other in a completely different light. The students will be surprised at how vulnerable some teachers will feel about learning a new skill, and the teachers will see a different side to the students. Enjoy!

Taking it further...

Why not enter some of your adult learners for the actual Grade 1 (or even Grade 2 or 3) exam? Some of them will enjoy the challenge.

Top tip

Keep the buzz about the Grade-1-a-thon going by visiting lessons to take photos/recordings and sharing them with the rest of the school community.

70 Staff ensembles

"This idea is great for staff well-being."

Are there teachers in other departments of your school who you know play instruments or sing? Why not get them together and form a school ensemble?

Top tip

There are plenty of reasons why you could or should start a staff band or choir. It could be that you need to boost your end-of-term concerts, or you want to raise the profile of the department in the school, *or* you genuinely want to contribute to staff well-being. Whatever the reason, a huge amount of fun and laughter will be guaranteed. Like your other extra-curricular groups, those involved should enjoy the music-making and there is no reason why you can't strive for high standards (but be realistic!).

Taking it further...

Get more staff on board and run a Grade-1-a-thon programme for a year. See Idea 69.

How often?

Realistically, staff (including you) are generally unable to commit to weekly rehearsals, so try and find a balance. If you can manage it once every two to four weeks, this is impressive. If you can, vary the day of your rehearsal each time, giving the opportunity for as many staff to attend as possible.

Repertoire

Finding music for your staff ensembles should be no different from finding music for your student ensembles. If you have a hotchpotch selection of instruments and abilities in your staff band, consider school arrangements such as *Kaleidoscope* in which there is a part for everyone (see Idea 62). If you are starting out with your staff choir, assess the group's ability by finding two-part arrangements and move on to more parts when you feel they are confident. Take (sensible) requests from them. Give them a sense of ownership.

Performing opportunities

Seeing teachers perform really puts them in a different light for the students. If you can include the staff band and choir in an end-of-term concert, that will go down really well with students and parents alike. If you are struggling to find performers for a school event and your staff ensembles are up for it, do it!

Primary links

"Making music together is the best way to make links with your primary feeder schools."

As well as providing primary students with different musical experiences, giving them an opportunity to see you in action will hopefully get them involved and, more importantly, will help them with their usual transition anxieties.

Workshops

The best kind of interaction is most certainly a workshop involving your students alongside the primary students. Select a class that you think will be up to the task. It might be a KS3 class, or more likely an older class. Select a focus. Singing? Instruments? If you are inviting or visiting a Year 6 class, then can you get some information about their musical ability and see what suits them best? You will probably have to lead the session, but if you ask your students to lead short activities and warm-ups, you will have the primary students eating out of your hand.

Concerts

Invite Year 6 students to attend an afternoon rehearsal. It could be chaotic but they will see the range of extra-curricular music you have on offer and it will inspire those who already play to begin a different instrument and those who don't to consider it. If you are feeling really brave then consider hosting a joint concert with one of your primary schools. Whatever the format, make sure that there is an opportunity for the primary students to play alongside your students.

Top tip

Finding the time to go out to primary schools or for them to come and visit can be difficult, so try and plan ahead as far as possible. Make sure that all parties are agreed in terms of the balance between performing/ workshopping and collaborating. See Idea 23 for more about transition.

Taking it further...

Why not host a regular Year 6 and 7 instrumental ensemble/choir with one of your feeder schools? Once a month after school, they can come to your school and rehearse together (possibly led by a sixth former) as part of your extra-curricular provision.

72 Inter-school relations

"In this day and age, it is good to expand your musical communities"

Having good relationships with colleagues in other local schools (and across the country) can only be a good thing. The possibilities arising from sharing resources and ideas are endless.

Taking it further...

If you are missing specific instrumentalists or voices in your ensembles, consider asking students from other schools to join. Be careful not to poach, and be sensitive to their existing commitments.

These days it is rare for music departments to work entirely on their own. With funding becoming an increasing issue for all schools, we often find our A-level classes being shared between partner or consortium schools. Your department may well be one who wants to forge relations with local schools or you may already do this. Whoever you are, consider the following:

Shared teaching

If you share your A-level teaching within each year group, then it is vital that you maintain a positive working relationship and regular communication. You will need to decide who is teaching which aspect of the course. Don't forget that music skills and knowledge will apply to all aspects of the course and the different papers (performing, listening, composing) should not be taught in complete isolation. Keeping a shared log of what has been covered each month will be helpful and will ensure that you are covering the whole course without treading on each other's toes.

Your teaching approaches may differ between the schools, but expectations must not. Think about whether your homework expectations the same. What will happen if work is not acceptable or needs redoing? Who is responsible for any sanctions that may need to be given? You need to be clear on this and it needs to be communicated to your students.

Local TeachMeets

Often there may be only one or two members of staff in a music department, and they can feel quite isolated. TeachMeets can be a great solution. If local networks don't already exist, then set one up. Host an informal after-school session where you can get local music teachers together to thrash out ideas, have a bit of a moan (try not to do too much of this), or even just chat (provide cake and people will come running). Hopefully you will come out of it with everyone's email address and it will be comforting to know you have contact with local colleagues to whom you can turn for support, either in person or via email.

Concerts

If you really want to bring the students together, a joint concert in the local concert venue or theatre will do just that. Each school brings a contribution from their department, and then all perform something together. Invite the local youth orchestra to come and play too, and programme a large work, perhaps with the youth orchestra accompanying and all the schools providing the singers.

73 Music hubs

"Music hubs work with schools to ensure all students get the best possible music education."

Traditionally, hubs are seen as 'the place the peris come from' (see Idea 87). This idea is designed to get you thinking more broadly about the role of hubs, and their relationship with your school and students.

Let's investigate some approaches to working with music hubs at secondary school level:

O Funding: Many hubs offer secondary school grants, from a few hundred to thousands of pounds. If your hub isn't offering any funding, ask them why not. If you need a new samba kit, or want to fund members of staff to run more ensembles, this money could be a huge help.

O Financial support: Hubs offer instrument loan-assisted purchase for students, and hire of full-class percussion sets. They also offer remission of tuition fees for low-income families. Make people aware of these schemes and take advantage of them.

O Workshops and training: Many hubs run cheap, or even free, training sessions, e.g. on singing in lessons, teaching theory, or running ensembles. They also offer a variety of music workshops for you and your students.

O Ensembles: Hubs run area ensembles that your students can attend. *Some* hubs are accused of poaching the best students for their ensembles, and not giving anything back to the schools. Make hub ensembles work for you. If you are a small department, send students to the hub ensembles for experiences you can't provide. If you are a growing department, work with the hub ensembles to inspire more students to take up instruments, sing and join clubs. If you are a huge department who thinks they 'don't need' the hubs, think more carefully. How valuable could it be if you join forces with hub ensembles for a project?

Top tip

The Ofsted publication *Music in schools: what hubs must do* is a useful read to check you are getting the most out of your hub.

Taking it further...

How could hubs benefit you as a practitioner? Could you lead a workshop for teachers or students for extra income or experience? Could you run an ensemble? Could you become a curriculum or teaching and learning advisor across your hub's schools?

National music initiatives 74

"Get your department on the map!"

The number of youth music initiatives on offer throughout the country can be overwhelming; the list below is by no means exhaustive but will hopefully give you a nudge in the right direction.

Music for Youth
(mfy.org.uk) @musicforyouth

Music for Youth is a music education charity, dedicated to 'providing free access to performing and audience opportunities for young musicians across the UK' (mfy.org.uk). Apply to be in the audience for one of their numerous events, or apply to take part in one. The Music for Youth Schools Prom is a well-attended three-day concert series in the Royal Albert Hall, which showcases young ensembles from throughout the UK.

Youth Music
(youthmusic.org.uk) @youthmusic

This is another 'national charity investing in music-making projects for children and young people facing challenging circumstances'. **(youthmusic.org.uk)** Go to their website to find out about the huge number of projects they have on offer.

Friday Afternoons
(fridayafternoonsmusic.co.uk) @fridaypms

Friday Afternoons started as a celebration of Benjamin Britten's 100th birthday, creating a national event to get as many young people around the world to sing. Each year in November there is now a massed singing event for which schools and youth organisations can download commissioned works for young voices and take part from their schools.

Taking it further...

If you don't have a Twitter account (and by the time you have finished this book, we hope you will have!) then sign up and start following organisations such as these. It will open up all sorts of doors for you. Tweeting them (especially from your department account) is a good way to become noticed and recognised.

Bonus idea

Enter your ensembles or advanced soloists for local and national competitions. Make sure they see them as opportunities to perform in different venues and circumstances rather than focussing on the competition element. Any prizes will be an added bonus!

75 Boosting KS4 numbers

"How to grow your GCSE and BTEC numbers?"

Music, along with other arts subjects, is often 'under threat' when it comes to numbers at KS4. Parents and students are concerned with EBaccs, university places, and 'a broad and balanced' curriculum, and can easily forget that students should be studying what they love.

Top tip

Our job is to help students understand that music is a fulfilling subject, and one that stands alone on merit. If students need 'how does music help me' posters and career paths, bite the bullet and grab the sticky tape.

Bonus idea

Bodies such as the Cultural Learning Alliance (**culturallearning alliance.org.uk**), the Arts Council (**artscouncil.org. uk**), or Music Mark (**musicmark.org.uk**) can help you prove the value of music to students, parents or SLT! Visit their websites for more information.

Target particular students

'Wine and dine' those who may not see music as an obvious choice, but should be pursuing the subject further. Take them to concerts or workshops, feature them in extra-curricular ensembles, and get them thinking about a GCSE or other qualification in music.

Make sure your results are top-notch

Numbers and percentages speak loudly on options evenings. Make sure your figures show that your teaching gets results.

Quotes from former students

Students will respond to the words of their peers, so collate feedback from them or invite them along to talk to prospective students on open days.

Music is for everyone

Make sure students with a background in *every* type of music can see that Music GCSE (or equivalent) is for them. Find examples of work from across the genres to show students and parents you talk to.

Make sure KS3 is engaging and exciting

A KS3 curriculum that includes exciting performing, composing and listening activities, that engages students and enthuses them when making music, will inevitably lead to healthier KS4 numbers.

Boosting extra-curricular **76** numbers

'Shall I start from Year 7 and build up...?'

You can't just assume you can grow your extra-curricular groups up from Year 7. They will inevitably drop off in numbers in the older years, as their predecessors have done. Try these ideas to help keep the numbers up.

Get the older ones back on board

They are all lurking there somewhere. Butter them up. Personally invite them to an ensemble, explaining how much you would like them to take a leading role in the ensemble, and that the lower school needs them. Chase them up if they don't come and ask them to at least give it a chance.

Make sure that they are playing a lot in the first rehearsal, and that the music is challenging enough for them. Ask them to take a sectional or small group if appropriate and then ask their opinion at the end. Is the repertoire suitable for everyone? Do you think this will sound good? Of course you know what the answers are, but making your students feel included in decision-making will no doubt encourage them to come to rehearsals each week. If your upper school are on board, the lower school will come running.

Repertoire (see Idea 52)

Combine music that appeals to everyone and sounds good quickly – probably simple popular music arrangements – with something which challenges them technically and musically so that they know you mean business. Involve them in decisions without letting them take over.

Flagship ensembles (see Idea 60)

Creating chamber ensembles for which students have to audition means that you can really challenge your more able students, setting high standards to which other students in the department can aspire.

> **Top tip**
>
> Arrange for one of your groups to perform at a school event (avoiding assemblies as students often have huge issues performing to their peers in such a formal setting). It could be a short slot at the school Christmas fair, or even at the AGM of the parents' association. Getting them out into the community shows that you have confidence in their performances and that you are proud of them.

77 Developing role models

"When I grow up, I want to be like..."

Whether they are conscious of it or not, younger students are always looking up to the older year groups in the department and around the school. If your older students become less active in extra-curricular music as they go up the school, you can't expect your (currently) enthusiastic Year 7s and Year 8s to be any different.

Maintaining enthusiasm for extra-curricular music in your upper school is key to a successful and thriving department, but how?

Auditioned groups and expectations (see also Idea 60)

It is sometimes the case that your older students may gain places in your flagship ensembles and then decide that they 'don't have time' for the larger non-auditioning groups. This can often lead to a two-tier system, where students gain some kind of misplaced superiority complex once they have 'made it' into an auditioned ensemble. Avoid this by putting some expectations in place. For example, all members of the chamber choir should be expected to remain in the main choir. They will raise the standard of performing around them and will be a friendly face to younger students. No one is too good for your big non-auditioning ensembles.

Student-led ensembles (see also Idea 63)

Giving students the responsibility for an ensemble and recruiting for it will challenge them, especially when they start taking rehearsals of their own. Be on hand to support them but try and let go as far as you can.

Top tip

Also try getting your older students to take registers, organise music and be responsible for general logistics at rehearsals and concerts. This will give them a sense of responsibility whilst relieving you and your staff of a few jobs too.

Taking it further...

Turn your most dedicated and experienced students into music captains or prefects (see Idea 78).

Music captains 78

"Creating sixth-form music captains benefits them and you!"

Having music captains is similar to the traditional prefect system; sixth formers take a lead role in the music department and provide a great link between the staff and students.

Your decision to appoint music captains may already fit in with a school-wide system, but if not, be brave and take the plunge as the rewards will be endless. Asking students to apply for the post will make sure that the students take the role seriously. As well as developing their own strengths, they can bring some new ideas to the department – for example, our school's woodwind ensemble and folk group came out of captain applications.

The types of responsibilities the captains take on often vary each year, according to students' strengths. Some will make superb accompanists, others great leaders of small ensembles, and others will be happy in the background keeping music and registers up-to-date. If your captains are exceptional musicians, asking them to run a small ensemble is the perfect way of stretching them, expanding on their musicianship skills in a completely different way.

As a team, the captains can take on projects together: maintaining displays, making a department video (great for showing on parents' evening), or even running a project, such as a Grade-1-a-thon (see Idea 69). When it comes to concerts, your captains can help with the organisation of rehearsals, ensuring that all students are in the right place at the right time, and leaving you time to worry about the music.

(see Idea 69)

Top tip

Providing sixth-form students with leadership opportunities not only develops their interpersonal skills, but they also become excellent role models for younger students. Giving them responsibility forces them to be organised and helps them to develop their communication skills with a wide range of people. All this as well as the added bonus of saving you time in areas they can help you with – it's a no-brainer!

Taking it further...

If this system is new for you, encourage another department, for example the drama department, to start the same system. The potential for cross-curricular projects would be huge!

79 Open evenings

"Not more text books, exercise books and posters!"

You are the one and only music department in the school. Music is the language of the classroom, and so it should be the language of your department on an open evening. Be strong, and don't put things on display for the sake of it.

On open evenings, by all means put out workbooks and folders and whatever your students use for record keeping, and make sure displays are looking impressive, but don't forget that most prospective parents and students will be looking at work like this in other departments all evening. They are unlikely to get any kind of flavour for your department by glancing briefly through books and folders. Consider the following ideas.

Student practical work

Taking it further...

Secure a slot for a live performance in the headteacher's speech. This is a great opportunity to showcase your department, as well as providing a suitable opening for the whole evening.

○ Set up a laptop/iPod connected to a number of headphones with some performances or compositions you have recorded in class from a range of key stages. Link the recordings to the written work. If there is a Year 8 blues assessment/tracking sheet with student annotations on, then provide some examples of what the students produced during their blues project.

○ At GCSE and A-level, as well as putting out relevant anthologies (if applicable), provide some listening examples of performances and compositions from recent years, along with scores of compositions or commentaries. Make sure you try and cover a wide ability range.

Displays

○ Try to avoid just pages and pages of work and music; if you've got scores of compositions, why not store the recordings online somewhere (Dropbox, Google Drive, SoundCloud) and create a QR code for them? Parents and students can then scan them and listen to them on their own devices, and can even save them for later.

● Get your music captains (see Idea 78) to take photos of your extra-curricular clubs in action (don't forget to check permissions).

● If you have had any significant events in the year, for example a music tour, big concert, etc., make sure that these displays are in a prominent position such as the foyer.

● Still got room? If you are doing enrichment work for students between Year 12 and 13, set them the task of filling an area with work.

● If you have very large walls, then consider putting up a display of your musical passions; favourite composers, musicians, albums, etc.

Music

It is essential that you strike a good balance here. Live music is really important, but don't forget, visitors will want to talk to you so make sure that the music is not overpowering, and that there is always a member of staff available to talk to parents. Consider:

● Small ensembles/groups of musicians on a rota in one of the classrooms, run by older students to ensure efficiency and professionalism are maintained.

● An open rehearsal of a small ensemble.

● Making instruments available for prospective students to try, for example keyboards with headphones (tip: lock the drumkit away!).

● Playing recordings of concerts.

Top tip

Make sure you use your students! Ask a selection of them to come and represent your department. The best indicator on this kind of evening is how passionate the students are, and how well they can connect with the visitors.

80 Making a professional CD

"A professional CD is perfect for capturing musical highlights."

Making a professional CD can be one of the most exhausting but most rewarding projects. You will put the students through their paces but the end result will be worth it.

Plan well in advance.

○ Preparation and repertoire: You will need a minimum of about six months lead up, with more intense rehearsals closer to the recording. Select repertoire that the group can perform well and that you think people will want to listen to. Don't forget, you want the CD to sell well.

Taking it further...

Launch your CD with a concert to continue to raise money. Sell your CD anywhere and everywhere, but don't forget to give a complimentary copy to the students involved and anyone who has helped along the way.

○ Licensing: As you will be selling your CD, you will need to obtain the performing rights from the Performing Rights Society. The Limited Manufacturing Licence is perfect for a school situation – there is a flat fee depending on the number of CDs produced and the running time of the CD. Find out more from **prsformusic.com**.

○ Bookings: Unless you can produce this all at school, you will need to book a recording engineer, a venue and a producer. They won't come cheaply so cost it all out before you get the students excited about it. The producer's job is to point out mistakes and make improvements between takes. (You can't hear everything yourself if you are conducting.) If you hire someone, make sure they understand how to work with students.

○ The CD itself: Save money by asking a sixth form photography student to take a couple of high-quality photos of the ensemble. You might be able to get a student to design the CD artwork for you as well. There will be plenty of places online who can mass-produce your CD. Units are often in 500s and the cost per unit often goes down with the more CDs you make.

"Alumni are your extended family!"

Alumni can play a huge part in raising the profile of your department, whether they have gone on to study music or not. Try and keep in touch with all your students when they fly the nest!

Alumni are some of the most approachable role models for your current students.

● Alumni members make the perfect display. Put up a photo of anyone who goes on to study music or work in the music industry. It inspires the current students and can raise aspirations.

● Continue to celebrate their achievements. If your alumni played a key part in your department, it is likely that they will go on to do the same at university. If they are hugely involved in the musical life of the university, a Twitter mention is always nice, and of course any huge roles they may get (conductors/directors of orchestras and opera societies, etc.) are certainly worthy of celebration.

● Use your alumni as contacts for your current students. It is likely that whatever your students choose to study at university, you will know an alumni student who is doing that. They may exchange contact details to discuss applications, which may turn into coffee on interview day, etc.

● Ask your alumni to come and work with your students. For example, if they have continued to perform to a high level, can you ask them to lead some workshops? Or even run some seminars? Current students love hearing about experiences from people other than teachers!

Top tip

Keeping in touch with your students when they leave will probably be a very natural thing to do, and they will probably want to come back and see concerts and productions. If not, invite them. Having an 'alumni corner' at the back of the Winter concert is always heart-warming for the school community to see.

Bonus idea

Organise a one-off alumni event at school. It could be a joint choral or orchestral concert, or a battle of the bands. If there is an anniversary of the school or of a specific music ensemble, then mark it with a celebration concert/musical event.

82 Concerts in the community

"Take your students into the community — it's good for them!"

Giving your students opportunities to perform in venues outside school not only takes them to another level of performance – it's quite scary when 'real' people come and hear you perform – but does a huge amount to raise the profile of your department.

Try some of these ideas to get you started:

○ Churches: If your school has a tradition of a Christmas concert with carols, then consider turning it into a carol service in the local church. Apart from a bidding prayer at the beginning and end of the service, it is basically a selection of carols and readings, so hopefully people of all backgrounds will be able to take part if they wish to. Also, if your local church has a lunchtime concert series, see if you can be part of it once or twice a year. If you have a chamber choir who you think can handle it, consider introducing them to some Evensong repertoire. If you think they can't lead a service by themselves, get in touch with the choirmaster at your local church and see if they will consider a joint service.

○ Retirement homes: Again, Christmas is the perfect time of year to go and brighten up a retirement home, but most homes or day centres often have a programme of entertainment for their members throughout the year, and you could easily become part of the regular line-up. You could take a flagship ensemble, or take another small instrumental/vocal ensemble and soloists.

○ Local festivals and street parties: Often there are music (and non-musical) festivals which require a rota of musicians to perform throughout a day. Get involved: you never know, you and your students might even get a free ticket to the event.

Top tip

While this all sounds lovely and most exciting, be wary of overcommitting yourself and the students. You are all busy, so select your events wisely and don't forget that it's OK to say 'no' (see Idea 92).

"You will be surprised how many adults come out of the woodwork if you start advertising adult classes!"

If you have the time(!), setting up an adult choir, orchestra or even a music theatre group can only win brownie points for your department, especially when those involved see how much work goes into one of their sessions.

This idea can be so rewarding if you have the time. Here are some ideas to get you started:

○ Like any of your student ensembles, once you have a list of people attending (and the instruments they play and approximate ability), you can select appropriate music for them. Like your staff band or staff choir, start with simple arrangements which sound effective (see Ideas 52 and 70).

○ Team up with a drama teacher and form a musical theatre group. You do the vocal warm-ups, teach them songs from the shows, and the drama teacher blocks/choreographs the numbers. Make sure you choose songs from a variety of shows; eventually you will be able to work to the strengths of your group.

○ Like any ensemble, your adults will be keen to work towards some kind of performance. If you have room in your end-of-term concert, put them in! If not, someone within the group will surely know of local events taking place that might make appropriate performing opportunities for your choir or instrumental ensembles. With the musical theatre group, plan a showcase at the end of a series of classes: get some costumes and props and switch on that lighting rig! They will love it!

Top tip

Your sense of humour will need to shine through in these sessions, however good or bad your day has been. Don't forget that your adults will be coming as part of their relaxation time and, whilst they will want to get better, the most important thing they will probably want to do is have some fun.

Taking it further...

If your school runs after-school classes in other subjects, you may well find that you might even earn some money from the class too!

84 Little gems

"A little goes a long way."

The previous eight ideas have suggested ways to really raise the profile of your department. Some will be easy for you, others impossible, and some won't be appropriate for your particular department. There are however, smaller things you can do right away that involve less planning or financial investment.

Here a few little gems that can make a difference to the reputation of your department (in no particular order):

❍ Place posters and photos of concerts around the whole school, not just in the music department.

❍ Get a trumpeter(s) to perform *The Last Post* on November 11th, during the school's two-minute silence.

❍ Make a list of all the instruments members of staff can play, and display it somewhere around the school.

❍ Get some of your musicians to busk in the town centre, and make sure the name of your school is displayed clearly while they play.

❍ Provide music for the parents' association AGM, or a big meeting of the governing body.

❍ Get photos of your last concert on the front page of the school website.

❍ Get your music captains (see Idea 78), or older students to go into form groups, and advertise extra-curricular clubs. Get them to help out in KS3 lessons as well.

❍ Don't allow your blog or Twitter account to become dormant.

❍ Keep your department tidy.

❍ Be active outside music; get involved in house activities and sports or reading initiatives. Don't come across as an isolated department.

Taking it further...

To grow your department, you must strike the right balance between inclusivity and high standards. Make everyone welcome, but work them hard and get the best from them. That's all you can do at the end of the day.

"Where do I start as a new head of department?"

Every music department is unique. Every new subject leader inherits a different set of students and a different number (and quality) of ensembles. Take your time but have a vision.

When you have the time, consider the following in your new role as head of department:

● Teaching and learning is key. Even if you have just toured your latest production across the globe, if students aren't making progress in your lessons you are in trouble. Ensure that you, and your team, are delivering lessons in which the students are making music, making progress and appreciating your subject.

● Where are the gaps? Do you have strong instrumental ensembles but lack a great choir? Are there fewer boys involved, or fewer older students perhaps? Look to introduce new ensembles to fix this, or devote time to groups.

● What direction do you want to take your department in? You might want to promote jazz, classical or world music in your department. The best departments cover everything, but all departments specialise. Make clear to staff, students and parents what your department is going to look like. Don't do anything for the sake of it, or because you think it 'should' happen.

● Don't neglect results. Unfortunately, whilst school leaders love the kudos that a successful music department brings to a school (though we all know it is so much more than that), they will come down on you hard if your results aren't up to scratch. Ensure you are supporting students who need that bit of extra help, and stretching those who can achieve the top grades.

Top tip

Don't do it all at once. Creating a music department that is definitively yours takes time. Have a plan, stick to it, and communicate this plan with your team and those above you. Work tirelessly, but methodically, and don't try to do it all yourself.

Taking it further...

Countless other tips in this book are directly related to this one. Once you have decided on your 'direction' and 'focus', go back to the contents page and seek out what you need to know.

86 Your well-being

"I'm too busy to sit to down during the school day!"

Don't underestimate the importance of looking after your well-being. Teaching music is exhausting. You need to make time to eat and drink, exercise, and get out of the department. If you don't find time for yourself during the week, then the consequences for your well-being could be quite disastrous.

The demands on a music teacher are huge and you cannot sustain such a workload all year round without collapsing in a heap, unless you take steps to look after yourself.

Here are some simple ideas to help. We recommend that you *should* take on board at least one. You *could* take on board all of them!

Top tip

However difficult your day has been, don't forget to try and smile, especially at the students. If you've had a bad day, see the after-school rehearsal as an opportunity to make the day better, not an outlet for your frustrations.

 Get to the staffroom at break time: If you need to set up a lesson, do it as quickly as you can and then leave the department. Unless you have a student in absolute meltdown, then they can wait. If you can't avoid seeing a student, then make the meeting outside the staffroom so that you can go back in afterwards. Get a cup of tea and sit down with colleagues and talk about anything but the kids!

 Go for a short walk: At the end of the day (whether that be before or after rehearsals), take a short walk around the school. You can clear your head away from the department, and will probably bump into a friendly face and have a quick chat.

 Staff sport sessions: If your PE department runs staff sports sessions, take time out to attend. The exercise and sense of community will invigorate you!

○ Volunteer for working parties or teaching and learning groups: By joining even just one group, you will be spending time with different staff and contributing to something different. Throwing around ideas with them will be refreshing and you will be making a positive contribution to the school community in a non-musical way.

○ One or two free lunchtimes per week: Make sure you have at least one or two lunchtimes per week free of rehearsals. You might need to use this time to have informal meetings with students, or record the odd GCSE performance or composition, but it also might be time you use to go to the staffroom for lunch, or sort out your desk, etc.

○ Be sociable: Attend staff socials and take part in staff activities (Secret Santa is a classic). Getting to know your colleagues is a huge part of being happy at school. Relaxing with them away from the school environment will help you get to know them, and see them as part of your support network.

○ Cut-off time for evening work: Whichever way you work in the evenings, consider having a cut-off time. Try and give yourself some time to switch off, even if it is just 15 minutes in front of the TV.

Taking it further...

If you think there is something missing from the school's well-being network, start something up yourself (or with a colleague). You will be surprised at how many people have been waiting for you to start a staff book club/crocheting club/chess club.

87 Instrumental teachers

"How can a music department work efficiently and effectively with a team of peripatetic teachers?"

It is important to develop strong working relationships with your instrumental teachers. Good communication and organisation is key to building a dream team.

Here are some tips for organising your instrumental teachers:

❍ Produce a detailed and clear information pack that includes: procedures for timetabling lessons, reporting missed lessons, dress code, relevant whole-school rules and policies, contact details, key calendar dates, etc.

❍ Send regular emails to your instrumental team, giving reminders, new information and updates.

❍ Plan ahead – last-minute changes are rarely welcomed by instrumental teachers. They have a fluctuating income, so every missed lesson can impact hugely on them.

❍ Get admin support from a dedicated member of staff, or a member of the finance team. You *need* help with billing and parental contact.

❍ Using teachers provided by your hub means they will monitor teaching quality, and support you if issues arise. Prices are set by the hub (they usually take a cut for admin fees), and they will have schemes to help students who can't afford lessons. Employing private teachers gives you more freedom, in terms of finance and who you get in, but the admin, as well as the monitoring of quality, falls on you.

"I regularly need to tap into the school community."

Developing excellent working relationships with your support staff is key to you staying sane and happy. Teaching assistants, caretakers, finance and reprographics departments can all make your life so much easier!

Teaching assistants

This is easy. It goes without saying that if you need to use them in the lesson then give them an idea beforehand what they will need to do. Not many TAs are musically trained and get very nervous about supporting in music lessons. If you think that you don't need them, let them know in advance so they can support someone else.

Caretakers

Making friends with caretakers is essential! They will set out your chairs for concerts, move heavy instruments and make sure the school stays open for your evening events. They may even drive minibuses for you for external concerts. They are on hand for small repairs and odd jobs that you don't have time to do. They are an essential part of all event planning, so keep them in the loop and treat them well.

Finance

Running concert trips and tours is difficult enough without having to keep a tally of who has paid, etc. If you don't have a trips coordinator in your school, seek help from the finance office. In most cases, they will be able to take some jobs off you and collect money for you.

Reprographics

Keep on the right side of the person who does your photocopying. Get things to him or her in good time and ask if you can have some test copies of the programme in advance of a large photocopying job.

Bonus idea

Your school may employ a number of cover supervisors who will not always be used during all lessons. If they are known to be helpful, then approach them about small admin jobs that need doing. They might sort through some concert replies, or even begin to catalogue your extra-curricular music for you. It might not be regular, but any help they may be able to give would be gratefully received.

89 Managing your finances

"Money, money, money."

Music costs money. Instruments, instrumental lessons, and other equipment put a real strain on a department's budget. Here are a few ideas for saving and making a little extra money.

Saving money

○ Look after and store your equipment properly. If something breaks, try and fix it (by you, a technology department colleague, or a professional) before buying new.

○ Hire instruments from your local hub – this is a very effective way to keep costs down; you pay on a termly basis, so you can continually reassess what you need.

○ Enlist the help of your instrumental teachers. If they hear about an ex-display timpani, or a shop-soiled trumpet, ask them to let you know.

○ Store your extra-curricular music properly so you can use if again. Borrow from local schools or orchestras, swap with colleagues, and use your local library.

Making money

○ Don't feel bad if you want to charge for your concerts or put a bucket out at the end. And, if you think you could fill a larger hall, book it.

○ Make a professional CD, and sell it (see Idea 80.

○ Don't be afraid to ask for donations from local communities and businesses. The worst they can do is say no, and you might find a benefactor who just needed a little push.

○ Keep your eye out for funding opportunities and grants. Various arts organisations, and music hubs, offer funding for all sorts of projects.

○ Ask your parents' association to help you fund a specific project or purchase.

Taking it further...

Make the case to your SLT that you should be allocated additional funds for extra-curricular music, in addition to your department's budget. If they want the glory and prestige that comes with great concerts, they need to pay for it.

Bonus idea

In all the stress of not having enough cash, don't forget to give to others too. Christmas is the perfect time to give to charity – consider setting aside a portion of your Christmas concert takings to give to a charity of your students' choice.

Photocopying
dos and don'ts

"Am I allowed to make a photocopy of this?"

Photocopying in education is a much-disputed area. However, the Schools Printed Music Licence attempts to help schools struggling with dwindling budgets, while at the same time protecting copyright for artists.

Essentially, the new guidelines which came into force in 2013 significantly ease the pressures of money and administration for curriculum music. The key dos and don'ts according to the licence are detailed below:

○ You can photocopy music for use in classrooms, without having to contact the copyright holders directly.

○ You can edit and/or arrange the music, as long as you don't change the 'essence of the work'.

○ You can give out these photocopies to members of the school, as long as they are destroyed at the end of the school year.

○ You can use photocopied music in performances, but these performances cannot be recorded or broadcast (unless additional licences have been obtained).

○ Choral leaflets are specifically excluded from this. You will need to buy enough copies for your choir.

○ You can copy a maximum of ten percent of anthologies or multi-movement vocal works (one movement maximum for works with fewer than ten movements).

○ Copies made for private instrumental and vocal tuition are not covered.

○ There is a list of excluded works, e.g. grade pieces and some classroom workbooks.

Taking it further...

To see the complete details of the *Schools Printed Music Licence*, including excluded works, visit: **cla.co.uk/schools-printed-music-licence**.

Bonus idea

Make sure you check the restrictions and requirements in your exam board's specification, and the publisher's own rules for staging musicals.

91 Essential toolkit for music teachers

"I love this idea, it is like a shopping list for your desk!"

There are a few items music teachers just can't do without. Make sure the following bits and bobs are within arm's reach at all times, and you'll save yourself a lot of stress.

Make sure you have these essential toolkit items to hand in your department:

○ Guitar essentials (picks, leads, strings, a capo and a clip-on tuner): Guitarists (generally electric guitarists) and 'faff' go together like macaroni and cheese. They can easily spend an entire lesson 'setting up their amp', and even then will come and ask for something they should definitely have. Having a range of guitar accessories to hand will reduce your blood pressure. The clip-on tuner has other uses, but guitarists will need it the most.

○ Beaters and drumsticks: There is a mythical gnome who visits music departments in the dead of night, and steals drumsticks. Don't try and trap him, just buy a load of beaters and sticks and have them close at hand.

○ Adaptors and splitters: 'Big to small', 'small to big', and 'two small to one big'. This is the language students use to describe 3.5 mm to 1.4 inch adaptors and the like. They are used to put different types of headphones into your keyboards and computers. Always over-order.

Bonus idea !

It is important to label your stuff. It makes it more likely that it will stay in your department. Rather than a bland label, try neon tape. It makes it easier to see, looks cool, and you can just wrap it around everything you own.

○ Screwdrivers, sticky tape and duct tape: 99.9% of quick repairs can be sorted with these basic tools. Anything else will require a trained professional.

○ Manuscript and tab paper: You can download these for free, print and then and photocopy them.

○ Spare reeds: For reed instruments, in an emergency.

○ A drum key: Drummers always ask for this. They know what to do with it.

Knowing when to say no

"It's just one event too far!"

If you are feeling overloaded with coursework deadlines and concerts both in and out of school, how will you decide what to shelve or which events need to be turned down?

Work deadlines

These are the most important and can't be moved, so they must be prioritised. If it is this aspect that is stressing you out, then you should consider the points below...

Rehearsals

If you are coming up to a really busy period, then consider pausing an extra-curricular club or two for a very short time. Students will understand, especially if you rehearse regularly throughout the year. You never know, they may be relieved to have some time too. If you can't bear it, consider making a rehearsal shorter or even change to rehearsing every two weeks. If there are suitable sixth formers who could run the occasional rehearsal, then give them some responsibility. They will love it!

Concerts and events

In your busiest period, you've been asked to provide some music for an event, which will involve you selecting one of your smaller ensembles and ensuring they have enough repertoire and are up to performance standard. What is your response? When you are really busy and are deciding which events and concerts to do, consider the *musical value* for the students. Will they gain anything from the experience or are they simply providing some incidental music? If you think it will be a great musical experience for the students, and you *could* probably squeeze it in, then go for it. If you think it might just be providing some incidental music and the students can manage without you, then ask some sixth formers to cover it. And if another request is simply the nail in the coffin, then just say no!

Top tip

No one will hold it against you you for saying no to things, but soften the blow with an alternative offer: if you can't put on a concert in the local church this term, can you fix a date for later on in the year?

93 Making an impact as an NQT

"How do I hit the ground running?"

You have joined your first school. What should you be looking to achieve, and what should you be looking to get out of your first year as a teacher?

DOs

○ Extra-curricular ensembles: Run one ensemble, and start a new one. You might well wish to do more, but it's a start. Be careful not to step on any toes (so don't go for the flagship ensembles in your first year). Your new club could be a feeder group for an established ensemble or something completely different that the department has never seen before!

○ Design a scheme of work: If there is a unit that is tired, offer to design a new one. Make it an engaging unit with clear progression and one that all the members of your department can teach. Provide a complete set of resources and lesson outlines. You will be popular.

○ Offer to run sessions for underachieving students: This is a perfect way for you to help the department, make a difference, and improve your teaching skills.

○ Do something outside your department: Make sure it isn't a huge drain on your time. Getting out into the wider school community will help you make friends, catch the eye of other members of staff, and ensure you don't get under the feet of your head of department.

Taking it further...

Your school should have a member of staff in charge of NQTs. You need to know who they are, and how they can help you. They should be organising training sessions in school, and should allow you to access CPD outside of school.

○ **Constantly reflect on your practice:** This doesn't mean beating yourself up after every bad lesson or rehearsal. Just make a mental or written note of what went well, and what you could do better. Put this into practice the following day, week, month or year.

DON'Ts

○ **Don't be pushy:** You might have great ideas, but you aren't in charge. Offer your opinion, and make suggestions, but accept it when you are overruled. When you have your own department, you get to make the decisions.

○ **Don't get pushed around:** Your head of department is busy, so should be delegating to you, but he or she should also be reasonable. You need to say no when it gets too much. Have a conversation with your head of department first, and go to your link SLT member if that doesn't work.

○ **Don't burn yourself out:** You don't need to reinvent everything the department does (at least not straight away!). Do a few things well. Keep your friends, your social life and your hobbies. Most importantly, don't stop being a musician.

○ **Don't be someone you are not:** *Never smile before Christmas* is absolute rubbish; if you are goofy, be goofy. If you are quiet and kind, be quiet and kind. If you are a natural disciplinarian, do that. Be professional, but be yourself.

○ **Don't be late and don't miss deadlines:** Be organised and be on your game. Get the basics right.

Bonus idea

Get support. There will be many others going through the same highs and lows as you. Keep in touch with colleagues from your training year, and join the variety of support networks on Facebook and Twitter.

94 Out-of-house professional development

"Always keep in mind your continuing professional development."

All teachers should always be looking to develop and improve their practice, and learn new things. Much of what you do in school contributes to your CPD, but there are valuable opportunities available outside of your department too.

Out-of-house professional development can take many forms:

◗ Visiting another school: Visiting another school can be great for picking up new ideas. Make sure you know they have something to offer you, and make sure they know what you are hoping to get out of the day as well. Also, take something with you to give to them (sharing is caring).

◗ Attending courses run by external companies: Many companies offer specific courses on things like composition, harmony or the individual components of an exam boards' qualification. These courses can be fantastic, filled with exemplar material and real examiner feedback, giving you a really focussed sense of how to adapt your teaching on your return.

Bonus idea

Musical Futures runs the Wednesday night twitter discussion #mufuchat. Whether you take part in the debate, just observe, or read the pre- and post-chat forums, there is always something for every music teacher to take away from these sessions.

◗ Conferences and exhibitions: These have a mix of workshop, seminars and lectures as CPD and often also have the opportunity to visit stalls run by different retailers. One such exhibition is the *Music Ed Expo*, run by Rhinegold. It takes place over two days and advertises itself as 'free, high-quality CPD for music and performing arts teachers'. Also check out the National Association for Music Education conferences and the Music Mark annual conference.

◗ Workshops: Workshops can take many forms and be on varied topics, from conducting choirs to delivering new specifications. Look for free workshops run by your music hub (see Idea 73) or organisations such as *Musical Futures* (see Idea 10).

Sharing good practice

"For it is in giving that we receive." (St. Francis of Assisi)

Get online and make the most of the resources and forums out there. But don't forget to contribute yourself!

There are countless forums for teachers online; Facebook groups, Twitter and chatrooms are goldmines for ideas, resources and strategies. But don't just read what others have done, or steal resources without contributing something yourself.

Alongside your class or department blogs and Twitter accounts, why not maintain a professional, personal account? You could simply re-tweet articles and links or write about things you have tried in class, approaches you have taken, or resources you have used. You could share the resources you make for your students, in the hope that others will find them useful.

Generally speaking, resources tend to come from two places: exam boards and huge publishing companies, or small independent developers, often working on their own. The former produce great resources, have huge marketing departments, and charge accordingly. The latter work from their studies or bedrooms, and charge small fees that usually only cover costs. They rely on word-of-mouth to get their resources out there. If you find something you like, and don't think many people know about it, tell people! Tweet about it, talk about it in the staffroom, or write a blog post. For example, I think that David Riley's 'Triptico' (**tripticoplus.com**) is an amazing collection of resources for all teachers, so I am telling you about it!

Top tip

Sharing is good. Many teachers share because they are good people, and because they want to make the world a better place. It can also enhance your professional reputation. It can lead to a secondary stream of income; a popular blog can generate advertising revenue, or you could be asked to write articles for magazines or other publications.

Taking it further...

A great way to pass on your knowledge, skills and experience is to train the teachers of tomorrow. Take on a trainee teacher if you possibly can (see Idea 96).

96 Teacher training

"Training tomorrow's teachers can be very rewarding!"

As well as supporting them in their training, taking on a trainee will often bring new ideas to a department, an extra pair of hands and may even keep you up to date on current pedagogical thought.

Here are some tips for getting the most out of working with trainee teachers:

○ Lead by example: Your trainee will observe you and your colleagues for a period of time before being phased into the classroom. Ensure that your trainee sees a variety of key stages and staff. Your job is not to produce a clone of you but to help the trainee find their own teaching style. Encourage them to try out ideas, even if you know that some of them may not work with your students.

○ Share and share alike: You will, of course, give your trainee access to all your department's resources for all key stages, but a good trainee will want to write his or her own resources as well. If they don't, then ask them to create some resources for some of your schemes of work (and make sure they leave you a copy). If they are expected to devise a scheme of work as part of their training, offer support and guide them through the writing process.

○ Extra-curricular: This is where your trainee could be invaluable. If they are up to it, then ask them to run an ensemble. They may have other ideas about what they could bring to the department as well. Make use of their vocal and instrumental skills by asking them to attend one or two other extra-curricular ensembles as support. They can take sectionals or simply add to the confidence of the existing students. Do be careful not to overload them though; they are still learning and will need time and space.

Top tip

In most cases, the benefits of having a trainee in the department most certainly outweigh any reservations you may have. If you end up with someone who requires more support than you can offer, however, make sure you have support in place too. Contact your school professional mentor and seek help.

Department blocks

"I couldn't remember the name of the piece of music you told me to listen to for homework!"

Blogging is a great (and free!) way to share homework, wider listening and department information with your students. The students do not require any login details, the information is readily available from all devices, and students can take ownership of their own organisation and learning.

There are a variety of blogging platforms which are generally quite intuitive and user-friendly. Decide which one is for you (Blogger is nice and simple, but WordPress looks a bit more professional) and give yourself a sensible and memorable address. Consider what kind of information or resources you will blog and then stick to it. You can choose who sees your blog or make it entirely public. If you choose the latter, don't forget to check your school's policy on students' photos.

You might think about blogging the following:

- listening resources for specific lessons

- homework

- wider listening and reading (YouTube videos can easily be embedded into posts, as can Spotify playlists)

- extra-curricular rehearsal and concert information

- information about concerts

- opportunities in ensembles outside of school.

If it all seems rather overwhelming, then try selecting one of the above and trial it with a specific year group. You can then expand it to a wider audience when you feel ready.

Be persistent: blog little and often and avoid replicating the information in another format (for example, paper) so that your students have no choice but to check your blog. Make the posts attractive to the students by including pictures and videos where relevant.

Top tip

Link your blog to a Twitter account (**twitterfeed.com**) if you want to reach a wider audience.

Taking it further...

Consider setting up blogs for each of your classes in which you can share recordings and work. An excellent example is **mrsgowersclasses. wordpress.com**. Although this website is no longer active, it is an excellent collection of work from 2011–2015.

98 Tweet your students

"But Miss, my tutor didn't read out any of the music notices yesterday…"

Twitter is one of the quickest and easiest ways of getting messages to students and parents. Reminders to bring instruments to the next lesson, rehearsal times, etc. can be tweeted to your followers. Get started today!

Here is a step-by-step guide to getting started:

Step 1: Consult your SLT about starting up a department Twitter account. Your school will have an e-safety policy and a certain amount of protocol which you will need to consider. If the response is a resounding 'no', do not give up. Collate some accounts from below which you can present as evidence of how it works at other schools.

Step 2: Set up your account. Most departments twitter handles follow the format: @NameofSchoolNameofDepartment

Step 3: Start following local and national accounts of interest, your local hub, youth orchestras and choirs, national ensembles (both youth and professional) and keep in touch with what's going on. Re-tweet (RT) tweets of interest to generate interest in your own account.

Step 4: Tell the students to follow you or just check your Twitter page; they don't have to sign up to be able to do this. Make sure you tweet useful information that the students need. Consider removing other ways of getting messages to them (especially if they are ineffective) so that your line becomes 'I'll tweet what you need for next lesson' or 'I tweeted that yesterday so you should have seen it!' It takes some time to embed but once you have built up a following, you will begin to feel the benefits. Students have the option of tweeting you short questions too, which can also be helpful.

Top tip

Building up a following outside the school community often leads to other performing and workshop opportunities for the students and, of course, contributes to raising the profile of your department. You can start by following @BeaumontMusic.

Taking it further…

If your department has a blog or website, consider linking it to your Twitter account so that when you post something, it automatically feeds through to your Twitter account.

Becoming a lead practitioner

"Become an expert in your field."

The process of becoming accredited as a lead practitioner is fantastic CPD, particularly if you have your eyes on an SLT role in the future.

The role of lead practitioner gives teachers an opportunity to become accredited as outstanding in their subject (correct at time of publication). Formerly known as Advanced Skills Teacher (AST) and, more recently, Excellent Teacher, the accreditation will give you an opportunity to share your outstanding practice (in order to improve student progress) in your school community and beyond. You will also be moved into the lead practitioner pay spine.

As well as being of personal benefit to you, being a lead practitioner brings a wealth of expertise to your school. Your school can ask you to lead training or observe a variety of teachers, thus benefitting your colleagues as well.

The programme involves a 'rigorous process of self-reflection and evaluation' (**ssatuk. co.uk**) and is made up of a 'framework of professional standards', which must be fulfilled by the teacher.

Like anything, there is a cost for the programme, which would be significantly reduced if you apply as part of a cohort. If you are interested, make sure you ask the relevant member of SLT who will be able to give you more specific answers.

Taking it further...

If you are inspired by further study and deepening your understanding of an aspect of education, consider investigating a part-time Masters degree in education. Or, if you have links with local universities, some will provide opportunities for action research projects which lead to Masters credits.

100 Music teaching – uncut!

"I love watching the out-takes at the ends of movies — it is so reassuring to see that everyone makes mistakes!"

A great music department is one in which students (and staff) feel comfortable enough to try things and make mistakes; one that sees mistakes as a learning opportunity. As in all good films, there will be bloopers along the way.

It is impossible to conceive of a department where every lesson is perfect – all students are engaged in the topic, making progress, being musical and learning. We can strive for perfection, but perfection doesn't exist in education.

Likewise, not every rehearsal or concert will be flawless. That is the nature of extra-curricular music. Passion and commitment from your students is more important than technical accuracy (but make sure they play or sing some of the right notes).

Here are some lesson time and rehearsal bloopers to make you smile and recognise that things do not always go according to plan in the uncut version of life as a music teacher...

○ You set your students up on a task, and barely get round any of the groups by the time the bell has gone.

○ A group doesn't really get started due to a malfunctioning keyboard/ computer/maraca.

○ A spider/leaking pen/sneeze/gust of wind destroys your perfectly conceived starter.

○ Every group's music is terrible.

○ You, or your students, forget how to count to four!

○ Most of your orchestra don't turn up because of a last-minute fixture change/ exam/change of venue/cake sale.

○ Someone breaks a drum kit/violin/window while transporting equipment from one un-ideal rehearsal space to another.

○ You accidentally spill coffee on a timpani or impale someone with your conductor's baton.

Top tip

A sense of humour and a sense of perspective are so important in education. Don't beat yourself up too much when things go wrong – give yourself a break. As Robert Burns said: 'The best laid plans of mice and men often go awry.'